Frederic Kidder, William Frederick Poole, Edward Ballard

The Popham colony:

a discussion of its historical claims, with a bibliography of the subject

Frederic Kidder, William Frederick Poole, Edward Ballard

The Popham colony:
a discussion of its historical claims, with a bibliography of the subject

ISBN/EAN: 9783337718343

Printed in Europe, USA, Canada, Australia, Japan

Cover: Foto ©ninafisch / pixelio.de

More available books at **www.hansebooks.com**

THE POPHAM COLONY

A DISCUSSION OF ITS HISTORICAL CLAIMS

WITH A

BIBLIOGRAPHY OF THE SUBJECT

BOSTON

WIGGIN AND LUNT, 13 SCHOOL STREET

1866

Edition, Three Hundred Copies.

BOSTON: PRESS OF ALFRED MUDGE & SON.

PUBLISHERS' ADVERTISEMENT.

In the following discussion, the arguments for and against the historical claims of the English Colony that landed at the mouth of the Kennebec River, August 19, (O. S.) 1607, are presented in an able and comprehensive manner. The articles, when they appeared in the columns of a daily newspaper, attracted much attention; and, as they contain matter of permanent historical interest, we have deemed them worthy of preservation in a collected form.

The writers can have no further motive for withholding their names. We therefore state that " P." is Mr. WILLIAM FREDERICK POOLE, Librarian of the Boston Athenæum; that "Sabino" is Rev. EDWARD BALLARD, D. D., of Brunswick. Me.; and that " Orient" and "Sagadahoc" are the signatures of Mr. FREDERIC KIDDER, of Boston.

Each year, since the first Popham Celebration in 1862, memorial services have been held on the Anniversary of the Landing in 1607. Public addresses have been delivered on these occasions, and these have usually been printed. Mr. John A. Poor, of Portland, Me., delivered the Oration in 1862; Mr. George Folsom, of New York, in 1863; Mr. Edward E. Bourne, of Kennebunk, Maine, in 1864; and Prof. James W. Patterson, of Dartmouth College, in 1865.

This discussion arose from a notice by Mr. Poole, in the Boston Daily Advertiser of April 11, 1866, of Prof. Patterson's Address which appeared about that time in print. In this notice the writer sharply assailed the claims for the Popham Colony, as set forth by the orator, and also by Mr. Kidder in a Letter

4

which the Publishing Committee of the Celebration had printed as an Appendix to the Address. Dr. Ballard replied in the Boston Daily Advertiser of April 21; and Mr. Kidder in the Portland Advertiser of April 26. From this point, the disputants came into close quarters on the general merits of the question.

As earnest historical discussion too often leads to bitterness and estrangement, we are happy to state that such has not been the result in this instance. "P.," whose notice brought on the discussion, received an official invitation to attend the Popham Celebration in August last, which he accepted. One of our firm, who was also present, can state that the hospitality of the Maine gentlemen named in the following extract from the report of the Celebration in the Boston Daily Advertiser, of September 1, is not over-stated :—

" I see to-day, among the guests from Massachusetts, your correspondent " P.," who has written of late some hard things respecting this Popham Colony. He is receiving every personal attention from Rev. Dr. Ballard, (" Sabino.") President Woods, Hon. Chas. J. Gilman and others ; and the merry peals of laughter, that burst occasionally from the group, indicate that difference of opinion on historical questions need not disturb the harmony of social intercourse. As I finish this report in Bath, I understand that Dr. Ballard and the other gentlemen named have captured their friendly detractor, and taken him home with them to Brunswick, where he will doubtless receive good treatment."

The Bibliography of the Popham Colony, which is appended, was compiled, at our request, by Mr. Poole ; and, so far as the newspaper articles, and the minor pieces connected with the first Celebration, are concerned, it was made chiefly from the collection preserved by Mr. John Wingate Thornton, of Boston, who has kindly placed them in our hands for that purpose. The list was then sent to Dr. Ballard, who has contributed the articles in his possession which were not already included.

W. & L.

[*Boston Daily Advertiser, April* 11, 1866.]

THE LAST POPHAM ADDRESS.

We find another contribution to the literature of Popham, in
the elegantly printed Address of the Hon. James W. Patterson,
delivered at the Peninsula of Sabino, on the 258th Popham Anniversary; which, as all the world knows without our giving the
information, was August 29, 1865. Thick, creamy paper, John
Wilson and Sons' best typography, and Mr. Wiggin's imprint,
were among the least of the motives that induced us to seize
upon and devour the contents of this delectable pamphlet.

We confess to a partiality for Popham literature. Its theory
is so original, so free from conventional trammels, so utterly at
variance with the accepted facts of history, that it is often difficult to persuade one's self that its advocates intend anything
more than historical waggery. So we read on, as in other fiction, to be amused.

A false theory zealously defended commonly finds more sympathy than the truth feebly supported. The Pophamites have
nailed their flag to the mast, and ask for no favors from any
quarter. We admire their pluck, and, for their sakes, regret
that they have so few historical verities in their ammunition
locker. We have read their "Memorial Volume," from title-
page to errata, as well as Mr. Poor's facetious Addenda in "Vindication of Sir Ferdinando Gorges;" not shying either at his
Appendix of fifty-two solid nonpareil pages. Every other Address on the subject, and every scrap of newspaper controversy
accessible, we have diligently perused; and yet the impression
remains on the mind that the facts to sustain this extraordinary

theory have not yet been developed. For some reason, (perhaps to surprise us the more when it does come,) the stern logic of truth is withheld; and we are served to empty assertion and vapid declamation in its stead. Every new publication, therefore, of Popham origin, or from the Maine Historical Society, is of interest, as possibly it may contain the suppressed developments. Plymouth and Massachusetts Bay are waiting, gracefully to yield the honors awarded them in history for more than two hundred years to " the Church Colony " of Sagadahoc. Is the pamphlet before us the coming document? Let us see.

Mr. Patterson is well known as a gentleman and a scholar. He has been Professor at Dartmouth College, and now is Representative in Congress from New Hampshire. Of his early local affinities we know nothing; but there was every reason to expect from him a valuable contribution to this historical discussion. His opening sentence is sonorous and impressive. " This [Fort Popham] is hallowed ground." Why " hallowed ground?" we would detain the Professor for a moment, meekly to inquire; but he hurries on to other glittering generalities. Is this spot " hallowed ground," because a colony of convicted felons landed here in August, 1607, more than half of whom deserted the next December, and all abandoned the spot the following Spring, leaving with the neighboring Indians the memory of the most shocking barbarities committed upon them? (See Relations des Jésuites, 1858, tom. i. p. 36; Parkman's Pioneers of France, p. 266.) Was it because these sportive colonists enticed friendly Indians into this same Fort, under the pretense of trade; and, causing them to take the drag-ropes of a loaded cannon, fired off the piece when the Indians were in line, and blew them to atoms? (See Williamson's Hist. of Maine, vol. i. p. 201.) " The lines of an eventful history," Mr Patterson goes on to say, " stretching through more than two centuries and a half, converge to this beautiful promontory of Sabino." We think not. Heaven spare the land from such a disgrace! Mr. Patterson devotes two pages to general assertions of similar import, and then branches off into another subject having no relation to the historical question. Into this we do not propose to follow him.

A curious feature in this pamphlet is an isolated Letter,[1] written by a respectable Boston gentleman, found in the Appendix. This alone, of the correspondence received by the Committee on Invitations, we are told, was found worthy of preservation. It was certainly not so much the name of the writer that rescued this letter from the oblivion of the waste-basket, common to its fellows, as the impression on the minds of the managers of the Celebration, that it contained historical information tending to confirm their theory.

The letter-writer finds that the "works" of the colonists, during the few months they stopped at Sabino, "were far more important than their formal acts recorded." The distinction he would make between "works" and "formal acts" is not quite apparent. Among the "works" he specifies, is "a vessel, the dimensions of which are unknown; but fit to cross the ocean." Strachey tells us what we know about this vessel. He says it was "a pretty Pynnace of about some thirty tonne." Whether it was fit to cross the ocean, we will presently consider. The writer claims for this fishing-boat the honor of being "the pioneer ship built in North America." This claim is nothing new. Mr. John A. Poor made it in Popham Memorial, (page 73,) and other writers of less *weight* have repeated it. The real fact, however, is that a vessel was built in the harbor of Port Royal (now Hilton Head) forty-four years before this, by Huguenot colonists, in which a party of more than twenty crossed the ocean. But, leaving out of the account the Huguenot vessel, a similar pinnace had been built at Sabino before this. Strachey says, under the date of 28th of August: "Most of the hands labored hard about the fort, and the carpenters about the buylding of a small pinnace, the president overseeing and applying every one to his worke." The other craft, called the "Virginia," for which the above pretensions are set up, was not framed till after Captain Davies had sailed for England,— that is, after the 15th of December.

The letter-writer further garnishes his theme by talking about this fishing-boat's "safe voyage to England," and the curiosity she excited in an English port. For the sake of these historical statements, the Committee have thought proper to preserve this letter. Their theory must be in a desperate condition to need such a confirmation.

We have a word to say with regard to this vessel. Writers on New England have generally stated that the departing colonists took this craft with them. This, however, is very different from the statements made above, that she was "fit to cross the ocean," that she made a "safe voyage to England," etc. A part of the company were not over anxious to re-visit their native land. They had saved their necks once by emigrating, and were not in haste to put them again into the halter. With this "pretty pynnace" they could catch codfish, and cure them along shore; barter them for other commodities with some of the hundreds of vessels from Europe employed in the fisheries on the coast; harass the Indians; and lead generally a wild and free life, such as was congenial to their character and dispositions. The vessels, doubtless, left Sabino at the same time. When the main body of the colonists departed, it was necessary that all should leave; for they had so incurred the enmity of the Indians by their barbarities, that any left behind would have been murdered. Strachey's account is entirely consistent with this. He says " they all ymbarqued in this new arrived ship [the 'Mary and John'] and in the new pynnace, the Virginia, and sett saile for England. And this was the end of that northerne colony uppon the river Sachadehoc." Brief Relation, 1622, says, "they built a pretty barke of their owne, which served them a good purpose, as easing them in their returning." Certainly; but we do not read that the "new pynnace" arrived in England, and was there an object of admiration, as a specimen of naval architecture.

The improbability that this "pynnace" was sea-worthy, and made a voyage across the Atlantic, will appear from the following considerations; —

1. There was not time between the 15th of December and Spring to build a sea-worthy vessel. There were but forty-five persons left in the colony, and this number was reduced before Spring by disease and squabbles with the Indians. There were probably not ten carpenters in the company. The Winter, we are told, was unseasonable and intensely severe. Strachey says, that, "after Capt. Davies's departure they fully finished the fort, trencht and fortified it with 12 pieces of ordnance, and built 50 howses, besides a church and a storehouse," — sufficient work, we might suppose, to employ forty-five Old Bailey convicts till Spring, without building a sea-going vessel. If Strachey does not tell the truth in this matter, we know nothing at all about this vessel.

2. They had no need of a sea-going vessel. These were furnished by the English undertakers. What they needed was a small craft in which to take fish along shore. The Huguenots built their vessel in 1563 to return home in; it being their only means of escaping starvation. There was no intention of abandoning the Popham settlement till Capt. Davies returned in the Spring with the news that their patron saint, Sir John Popham, surnamed "the hangman," was dead.

3. We know that the Popham colonists were knaves; but it is not necessary to infer that they were fools. Here was a good, stanch ship, the "Mary and John," of London, Captain Davies, master, about to sail for England. The whole company was now reduced to about forty souls. This same ship had brought over, a few months before, more than double that number. The graduates of penal institutions have usually as keen a regard for their corporal safety as other persons. Cowardice is commonly their ruling characteristic. Is it reasonable to suppose that any

of that godless company would have risked their lives to a voyage across the Atlantic in that "pretty pynnace," built of green pine, in midwinter, when they could have had safe and comfortable quarters in the "Mary and John"? If the intention, on the part of the managers, was to transport the colonists safely to England, there was no motive nor excuse for putting any on board the new craft. If there was a willingness on the part of some of the colonists to embark in it, they must, we think, have had some other project in view than a trip across the Atlantic. The assertion that the vessel made the voyage is purely gratuitous.

P.

[THE LETTER REFERRED TO ON PAGE 7.]

BOSTON, Aug. 27, 1865.

MY DEAR SIR, — Your invitation to be present at the Popham Celebration is at hand. The short notice will prevent me from being present to take part in the interesting ceremonies. Without assenting to all the claims made in your "Popham Memorial Volume," allow me to say, that I think those who have spoken or written on that subject have overlooked one of the most important results of that enterprise. In this practical age, we must look to what was really effected by the earliest colonists on these shores. Let us briefly try that at Sagadahoc by this test ; for, in my opinion, their works were far more important than the formal acts recorded. They certainly erected houses, a church, a fort ; and, lastly, a vessel, the dimensions of which are unknown, but fit to cross the ocean. Now we know, that, in a forest, it is not a difficult thing to build log-houses, or a church and a fort in the same way ; but to construct a sea-going vessel is quite a different affair. This requires artisans who are used to such work ; and there can be no doubt, that among the colonists there were found a master-builder,[1] with the necessary journeymen and sawyers (for there were no mills,) a smith, and also several laborers : for the building

---

[1] Strachey says, "the chief shipwright was one Digby, of London." He also speaks of "the carpenters." — Chap. x.

of a vessel in a remote wilderness would then require three times the amount of manual labor that would now effect the same result — in these days when materials are so easily prepared, transported and fitted, by the aid of machinery.

Looking, then, at what was certainly done by the Popham Colony, we must allow that, during the short period they occupied the rugged peninsula of Sabino, and making due allowance for a hard winter, the destruction of their store-house, and the sickness that followed, they deserve credit for enterprise and industry in constructing a vessel fit to encounter the storms of the Atlantic, and make a safe voyage to England. There she must have attracted much attention, being the pioneer ship built in North America. When, therefore, we consider the value of Popham's enterprise, the building and voyage of the "Virginia of Sagadahoc" is one of its most important results. It was not equalled by the Plymouth colony in the first ten years of its existence; and it was not till the third year of the existence of its powerful neighbor of "Massachusetts Bay," that a ship, fit to cross the ocean, was constructed.

Wishing you a pleasant day and a numerous company, I am,

Yours truly,

FREDERIC KIDDER.

To Rev. EDWARD BALLARD, *Secretary, &c.*

[*Boston Daily Advertiser, April* 21, 1866.]

"THE LAST POPHAM ADDRESS."

To the Editors of the Boston Daily Advertiser:—

By the courtesy of some unknown friend, I have received your paper of the 11th inst., containing a notice of Prof. Patterson's Address at the last Celebration at Fort Popham. As it presents some matters needing amendment, I trust your greater courtesy will allow space in your columns for a few observations.

Your correspondent has confessed a partiality for the literature growing out of the first colonial occupation of the soil of New England under English enterprise; and forthwith, in a style of pleasantry, bearing with it the edge of ridicule, speaks of the efforts of its writers as scarcely better than advocates indulging in " historical waggery," whose pages " we read," as in other fiction, " to be amused."

But without attempting to reply with smiles alone to such attempts at smiling away the force of historic verities, it is pertinent to say, that when your correspondent speaks of the " false theory " of the believers in the Popham Colony, it would have been quite as lucid a mode of treatment, if he had stated the " theory " itself. We had supposed that we were dealing with *facts;* and were not responsible for any deductions drawn therefrom, either by affection or prejudice. And the *facts,* though prominent, may be comprised in a short enumeration: That in 1607 an English colony, under President George Popham, was founded at the mouth of the Kennebec; — was inaugurated and continued with the sacred services of the Christian religion; — was an actual possession of the region afterwards known as New England, under a Royal Charter never denied nor abrogated; — and, though intended, as the documents show, to be perpetual, it came to an end within a year, by reason of the death of its two chief supporters; — and was followed by a succession of occupancies, that proved title, as against the former and never-renewed claims of France.

Now, if these facts make the " extraordinary theory," which your correspondent has not ventured to describe, we are ready to take it in all its dimensions, and furnish your readers the proofs, as readily as you will grant your columns. But we are not inclined to shut our mouths, or stop our pens, by the terror of any such words as " false and extraordinary theory," " empty assertion and vapid declamation." We do not ask " Plymouth and Massachusetts Bay gracefully to yield the honors of their exalted position," any farther than " the stern logic of truth " may demand; and we shall not be unwilling to say, that the claims of history are worthy of respect, even among the present dwellers in those ancient and time-honored colonies. As to the remark about "'the Church Colony' of Sagadahoc," that may pass as a piece of pleasantry, though it was a fact.

The question is asked, in regard to the opening sentence of Mr. Patterson's Address, "Why is this hallowed ground?" We had supposed, that any place where religion had held its services continuously, and in connection with important events, might properly bear such a designation. The orator evidently thought so; and his very large audience, out of the thousands assembled on that day, did not once think of a criticism upon the expression. But the question seems to have been proposed, not so much for disputing the religious associations connected with the undertaking, as to bring in *two* charges against the colonists, of no force whatever against the great purposes of the settlement.

The *first* charge is, that "a colony of convicted felons landed here in 1607." Now who believes this? We who live in the valley of the Kennebec have always supposed, that faith is belief founded on evidence; and that all other demands on faith, if answered, are credulity. What is the evidence that the charge is true? Not a particle. The only pretence of proof is the casual remark of Sir William Alexander, who says of these colonists, — of course he means the laboring part of their number, and not the ten in authority, — that they went to these western shores, "as endangered by the law, or their own necessities." But was there no other law than that against social crime? Contemporaneous history shows that their *endangerment* proceeded from the statutes against vagrancy. At that time, in consequence of the state of the country, a poor man could hardly avoid their grasp. Surely poverty was no crime. Gorges sought persons of this necessitous class to aid in carry-

1 Briefe Narration, Chap. ii.

[...] While Henry [...] of the Whigs, [...] The [...] to give the easiest [...] the best. They [...]

It is [...] on [...] for the truth of the charge about the felons, that Chalmers — and more to wit has had a [...] and [...] of searching the British State Papers of this period, and [...] the credit of being reliable as to facts — says the law for the transportation of convicts was not enforced till 1619, and Reeves says that when they were [...] the crimes of which they were convicted were chiefly political. The number transported to Virginia for social crimes was never considerable; scarcely enough to season the pride in its scorn of the laboring population; certainly not enough to affect its character. If there had been any convicts in the Kennebec Colony, it would be fair to infer from this declaration, that they were " chiefly political " offenders and " certainly not enough to affect its character."

But Chalmers says there was no transportation of any class of the guilty till 1619. Therefore there was none to Sagadahoc: and for the additional and better reason than his statement, that the law has not yet been shown requiring transportation as a punishment for moral guilt, during the time of the incipiency, continuance and end of the Popham Colony. Convicts could not be transported without a law. Any charge, therefore, as about the felons of the colony, is injuriously brought against the memory of the helpless dead.

The second charge comes from the cannon story: that the men at the fort induced the Indians to man the drag-ropes, and to stand in the line of direction of the piece aimed for execution: and then fired off the piece upon the whole body of

1 Hist. U. S., Vol. ii, p. 141.—Ed. 1857.
2 Political Annals, p. 48.

15

the unfortunates, when thus "in line, and blew them to atoms."
This is a tale of woe rather tougher than the quoted Williamson
gives it, — who is inclined to discredit it. But is even Williamson's reluctant account true?

The best reply to this allegation of horror is to be found in
the narrative of the Jesuits, in 1611, who went to the Kennebec
by the inland passage, in quest of corn. The Indians met them.
They gave them an account of their treatment of the colonists,
whom they represented as having been defeated by them. They
" flattered " the French, saying that "they loved them well;" and,
to gain their favor, told them how the English drove them from
their doors and tables with clubs, and made their dogs bite them.
All this might have been done for protection, under a renewal of
the hostile attitude assumed by the natives on Gilbert's trip up
the Androscoggin. The French were good listeners to any
charge against English Protestants. Now, if this story about
the cannon had been as true as its reality would have been cruel,
why should not these Indians have told its barbarities to such
good auditors? A cannon ball, with the explosion from the
muzzle, would have made a more damaging narrative than a club
or a dog-bite. Yet no syllable of the great event is recorded,
while the little ones are faithfully chronicled to the disparagement
of the Protestants. It is doubtful whether any cruelties did occur
so utterly at variance with the known kind treatment of them by
the " worthy " President. For the Jesuits say of these Indians,
that they were " flatterers," and " the greatest speech-makers
(*harangueurs*) in the world." When they had encouraged their
visitors (*honied* them, *emmieloyent*) with promises of grain, they
put them off by trucking in beaver.[1] Such witnesses do not
amount to much; and, if Mr. Parkman uses the language of your
correspondent in calling these uncertain incidents " the most

[1] Fuller information, gained from the military letters of Biard and Massé, shows that
the treatment referred to was connected with an occupation of the same location, by the
English, in the year *after* the Popham Colony had departed. — *Reports, edited by Carayon.*

shocking barbarities," it might be well wished that so able and interesting a historian as he, had given the brief narrative itself, rather than to have derived such a "theory" from its statements. Were there no "shocking barbarities" elsewhere against the natives?

The first known utterance of this cannon story was made in Massachusetts, about seventy years after its asserted occurrence. A few words may be allowed as to the letter in the Appendix, which comes in for a large share of notice. It is intimated that other letters were not worthy of preservation. The reason why they were not printed was because they were notes of courtesy to the Committee, not needing public expression. Mr. Kidder's letter was thought to have a historical value, as illustrating the skillful and industrious abilities of the colonists; and is certainly proved to be of some importance, or it would not have received so much attention.

The first criticism is verbal, on the non-apparent distinction between "works" and "formal acts recorded." To us, who have drank water, if not inspiration, from the still existent Popham well, beneath the shadow of Sabino Head, it appears that "formal acts recorded," were the acts of taking possession with chartered rights, placed on the minutes by "John Scammon, Secretary." The "works" were the daily toils of the laborers, in trenching, fortifying, building the storehouse and church and the "pretty pynnace."

We thank your correspondent for presenting the fact of a French vessel built at Port Royal forty years before any naval architecture was attempted at Sabino. We have been so much in the habit of thinking of English colonization, that perhaps we have had too narrow a horizon. But, better taught, hereafter we will be careful to put the patrial adjective as the proper predecessor, and say "the *English* · pioneer ship,'" and so again adhere to fact.

As to another "pynnace," built before this one claimed as the first, we are also glad to be assured of the fact for the first time. We had supposed that the two mentions, made in the Popham journal as given by Strachey, related to the one vessel, — in another writer called a " pretty bark."[1] But, if there were two, so much the better for Mr. Kidder's illustration touching the skill and energy of the colonists. Strachey says, they all embarked in the ship that arrived with supplies from England, "and in the new pynnace, the ' Virginia,' and set sail for England." This word *all*, used also by Gorges and Ogilby, and its equivalent by a contemporaneous writer, forbids utterly the statement of your correspondent, that a considerable portion of the colonists took the other " pynnace "—which we cannot yet see was built—to fish, and " lead generally a wild and free life."

It is also intimated that the " Virginia " did not reach England. But the " Briefe Relation," 1622, gives as much information about its arrival in England as about the arrival of the ship. A fair hearing of the old writer is enough to show that both reached the expected haven; and, doubtless, the first *English* vessel built in these wild regions did awaken curiosity in the beholders at home. But this may be " theory."

As to the improbability of the building of this vessel in the time allowed, and in the unusually cold winter, with the few men, it is enough to reply, that the " Briefe Relation " says this : " Having in the time of their abode there (notwithstanding the coldness of the season, and the small help they had,) built a pretty bark of their own, which served them to good purpose, as easing them [*i. e.* in the other vessel] in their returning."

The application of the term " hangman " is made to the Chief Justice Popham. But it is not easy to see what connection it has with the purpose of the colony. If the laws of the land required criminals to be hung, he cannot be blamed for their administration. Sad indeed will it be for magistrates, if they are to be thus designated because they execute the laws. It would not be

---

[1] Briefe Relation.

difficult to place his character in an honorable light, as he was
seen by his contemporaries; and as to his brother, George Popham, he has been truly styled by the historian of ancient Pemaquid, the "worthy" President, whom "New England counts as
among the earliest, if not the very first, of her 'illustrious
dead.'" SABINO.

[*Portland Advertiser, April 26, 1866.*]

"THE LAST POPHAM ADDRESS."

Under the above caption there was printed in the *Boston
Daily Advertiser* of the 11th instant, over the signature of "P.,"
what purports to be a review of Prof. Patterson's Address at the
Celebration of the two hundred and fifty-eighth Anniversary of
the Planting of the Popham Colony, at Sagadahoc.

At the first reading of this somewhat curious review, I supposed the writer had intended to throw ridicule on the Popham
celebrations, and all concerned in them; but, on a closer perusal,
I concluded that he has, to the extent of his abilities, really
undertaken to overthrow the whole history of that settlement,
and all that has been written about them, by the force of his
arguments.

He commences his theme by ridiculing the "Popham Memorial," the "Vindication of Gorges," and some other publications; but without attempting to reply to any part of them. He
next goes on to tell us that Mr. Patterson is a scholar, has
been a Professor at Dartmouth College, and is now a Member
of Congress; and then commences his onslaught by stating, that
on that spot (Sabino) a colony of convicted criminals landed in
1607, more than half of whom deserted the next December, and
the remainder left the next spring, after committing the most
shocking barbarities on the Indians; and refers to Williamson's

History of Maine, and Parkman's Pioneers, — neither of which authorities justify any such statement; and, although trying to ridicule some of Professor Patterson's sentiments, charges him with branching off into a subject that has no relation to the question at all.

Leaving the thirty odd pages of the Address without any remarks, he attacks a letter, written as a reply to an invitation to be present on that occasion, in which the writer notices the building of a ship by the colonists, as a fact of some importance, which, all the writers on that expedition say, took part of the colonists to England. But let us follow him through his many wild and unsupported assertions relating to that vessel. And here it may be proper to say, that the letter does not endorse the authors of the Popham Memorial, or any part of their theory, but at the outset expresses a dissent to many of the claims made by those writers, and refers almost entirely to the ship and its history. This reviewer, after some grand denunciations, finally concentrates his arguments into three stately propositions.

First, that the vessel never was built, because there was not time, and also that there was not over ten carpenters, or forty persons, in all the colony to do it, — while we know that since that day vessels of five times her size have been built with half that force, and in much less time, in that immediate vicinity. Second, that there was no need of a vessel; and third, that she was built of green pine, and no one would wish himself in her; and so the idea that she made the voyage is absurd. Now this is exactly the famous kettle argument over again, with results just as conclusive.

In reply to these three formal propositions, it is only necessary to say, that the fact of the building of the vessel rests on as good authority as any historical statement relating to that colony; that there were sufficient men and full time to do it in; and that there can be no doubt it was intended to build a ship when the expedition left England, from the fact that they brought out a master ship-builder and workmen. That she was built of "green pine" is an assumption very improbable, when we know that the growth along that shore was mainly hard wood, while pine predominates in the interior. But his most severe tirades are poured out upon the poor colonists, calling them felons, knaves, cowards, and almost exhausting the vocabulary of Billingsgate. To this I will not attempt to reply, but merely remark, that his language, style and logic, is as far removed from the "pure well of English undefiled" as a *pool* of stagnant water is from a perennial fountain.

A passing reader of his famous review would be at a loss to understand why this terrible onset is made on this small pamphlet, — nine-tenths of which he says does not refer to the Popham subject at all,— as though he expected to conquer them, Chinese-like, by only making a great noise. But a friend at my elbow says that this is a broadside in advance, or, rather, the fire of his skirmish line, and only preparatory to the advance of his big guns, which are to come in the shape of a preface to a reprint, in which he intended to entirely annihilate the Pophams, the Gorges, all their followers and biographers, great and small, rich and poor, so completely that our histories will have to be re-written, and these old names that have been so prominent in our early annals obliterated entirely; and finally to destroy the granite walls of Fort Popham, memorial stone and all, and by further displays of his cut-and-thrust logic prove conclusively that it is all a myth, and nothing of the kind ever existed. *Nous verrons.*

ORIENT.

[*Boston Daily Advertiser, May 31, 1866.*]

POPHAM AGAIN AND FINALLY.

Our notice of Professor Patterson's Address, in the *Advertiser* of the 11th of April, has drawn from "Sabino" an extended reply, which appeared ten days later. As our object in noticing the Address was not controversy; and as "Sabino," skirmishing here and there, has made no effective attack on any historical position taken in the criticism, we have doubted the propriety of making a rejoinder. The world is not in haste to become Pophamized. The memories and associations of more than two centuries, grounded on historic truth, are not to be pushed aside by the most absurd and baseless theory ever addressed to the human understanding.

"Sabino" has done us the honor of acknowledging, that we have contributed to this discussion some historical facts that had not before fallen under his notice, and he thanks us for the same. The most courteous acknowledgment we can make is, confessedly, a rejoinder. We shall therefore examine somewhat minutely several of the positions taken by our Eastern friend, hoping still to deserve his kind eulogium, by contributing other facts that may not have come within his observation.

We feel especially favored in having, as a disputant in this discussion, no amateur nor journeyman Pophamite; but the master-workman, the original inventor and patentee, the Magnus Apollo of the theory; he who compiled the "Memorial Volume;" who arranges annually those agreeable junketings, in midsummer, at Sabino Head; who is perpetual manager of the controversy and overseer of the press for all Popham publications. He kindly informs us (for no one knows so well as himself) why Mr. Kidder's letter was printed, confirming the impression expressed in our notice. Every fact and inference, favoring his side of the question that "Sabino" is not master of, is not worth knowing.

It is unfortunate that one so profound in Pophamistic lore should not express his ideas in clear and idiomatic English. Some of his sentences, after careful study, we confess our inability to understand; and he often makes use of words out of their ordinary meaning. For instance, he says, "We who live in the valley of the Kennebec have always supposed, that faith is belief founded in evidence; and that all other demands on faith, if answered, are credulity." How *demands* on faith can in any event be *credulity*, is to us as obscure as the metaphysical nomenclature in vogue in the valley of the Kennebec. Faith is defined by the best lexicographer of the language as "the assent of the mind to the truth of what is declared by another, resting on his authority or veracity, without other evidence." We, at the Bay, accept an older definition, running after this fashion: "Now faith is the substance of things hoped for, and the evidence of things not seen." We apprehend that if there is, in the valley of the Kennebec, any faith in the Popham theory, other than that held by our clerical friend and his copartners, it is grounded solely on the assertion of "Sabino & Co.," (the corporate style of the firm is the *Maine Historical Society*,) as something *to be hoped for*, but the evidence for which *is not seen*.

"Sabino," on the other hand, objects to our style, as not appropriate for a grave historical discussion. He is shocked that we should speak of his theorizing as "historical waggery, which we read, as we do other fiction, to be amused." Style, after all, is greatly a matter of taste, for which there is no accounting. We are now, however, to deal with History; and we promise our friend that our style shall be as rigid and matter-of-fact as he can desire.

"Sabino" complained that we commented on the Popham theory without "stating the theory itself." Our notice was written to be read only by those who are conversant with the historical discussions of the day, not one of whom, probably, is ignorant of what he and his Society have been doing and printing for the past four years. He supplied what he deemed an omission in our notice. We copy his carefully-prepared statement in full, and insert numerals, for convenience in its examination:—

"That in 1607 an English colony, under President George Popham, was founded (1) at the mouth of the Kennebec; — was inaugurated and continued with the sacred service of the Christian

religion (2) ; — was in actual possession of the region afterwards known as New England (3), under a royal charter never
denied nor abrogated (4) ; — and, though intended, as the documents show, to be perpetual, it came to an end within a year,
by reason of the death of its two chief supporters (5) ; — and was
followed by a succession of occupancies, that proved title, as
against the former and never-renewed claims of France " (6).

" These facts," " Sabino " says, " we are ready to take in all
their dimensions." " These facts," we, on the other hand, propose
to submit to a critical examination.

1. Was an English colony *founded* at the mouth of the Kennebec in 1607 ? An attempt was made then and there to found
such a colony ; but the speedy result of the experiment was a
disgraceful failure, and proved a warning to all future undertakers. This warning comes to us in the inimitable writings of
Lord Bacon. His lordship was personally conversant with the
circumstances ; and to him Strachey dedicates his " Historie of
Travaile," which contains the best contemporaneous account we
have of the affair. We quote from the first complete edition of
Lord Bacon's Essays, 1625, p. 199 :—

" It is a Shamefull and Vnbleffed Thing, to take the Scumme of
People, and Wicked, Condemned Men, to be the People with whom
you Plant: And not only fo, but it fpoileth the Plantation; For
they will euer liue like Rogues, and not fall to worke, but be Lazie,
and doe Mifchief, and fpend Victuals, and quickly weary, and then
Certifie ouer to their Country to the Difcredit of the Plantation."

" Sabino " shuns the usual expression " planted " for the more
pretentious " founded," as if the affair was a reality, and had a
foundation. A thing may be planted, and that be the end of it.
If the seed be bad, it rots in the hill. Such was the fact, and
fate of the Popham Colony.

2. The religious history of the Popham Colony is the briefest
narrative of the kind on record. All that is known of it may

be comprised in one sentence. A sermon was preached on two occasions; and some Indians were taken on a Sunday to the "place of public prayer," when they listened "with great reverence and silence." This conduct was highly commendable in the Indians; and, if the colonists, "the wicked, condemned men," had behaved as well, something, after all, might have come of the enterprise.

3. How much of "the region afterwards known as New England" was this Colony "in actual possession of"? A few acres of ground on the Promontory of Sabino, where they intrenched themselves, and nothing more! From this narrow foothold they were driven, on one occasion, by the Indians, who took possession of their Fort, their stock of provisions and military stores. Not understanding the nature of gunpowder, the Indians blew themselves up; and the survivors — regarding the explosion as an expression of disapproval on the part of the Great Spirit for their rudeness in driving, with arrows and clubs, forty-five Englishmen out of a Fort that was trenched, and mounted twelve pieces of ordnance — restored the premises to its gallant defenders, and proposed henceforth to live on terms of friendship. (See Williamson's History of Maine, i. p. 200.) Why does "Sabino" limit their possessions to New England? Why not give them North America, and the whole Western Continent?

4. The Popham theorists maintain, that King James's North Virginia Charter of 1606 had some special virtue as a barrier to French supremacy in New England. Both nations claimed the whole territory; — the English on the ground of Cabot's discovery, and of Gilbert's taking formal possession in 1583; and the French on the ground of prior settlement. The question of supremacy was to be determined by permanent occupancy, by enterprise, and by valor in arms; not by royal proclamations and charters. No royal charter to a trading company could strengthen the title England already possessed by right of

discovery and former occupation. The Plymouth Colony landed in New England without a charter, and the event will never be the less significant on that account.

5. The Popham Colony "came to an end within a year, by reason of the death of its two chief supporters." Did it ever occur to "Sabino," that his Colony must have had a very slender *foundation* to have fallen in ruins at the death of two, out of a hundred and twenty, persons engaged in it? The Plymouth Colony lost by death, in four months after the landing, fifty-one out of one hundred and two, and still the Colony lived. We neither accept nor deny "Sabino's" statement as to the cause by which *his* Colony came to its end. Mourners, in doubtful cases, should be allowed to settle these questions for themselves. It was a case of complicated diseases, any one of which would have resulted in dissolution. Sworn testimony and a coroner's jury would be necessary to determine the approximate cause. The first question before such a tribunal would be whether the patient could be said to have ever lived. Waiving this point, we should, if pressed for a verdict, give—"Died by visitation of the Almighty."

Who were the two persons whose lives were so intimately entwined with that of the Colony? They were George Popham, who came over as president, and his brother, Sir John Popham, who never came over — both very aged persons. Sir Ferdinando Gorges, who was "interested in all these misfortunes," and knew more of the end of the Colony than any other person whose writings have come down to us, did not regard the president's death as a matter of importance. He says, his death "was not so strange, in that he was well stricken in years before he went, and had long been an infirme man" (Briefe Narration, p. 10). Raleigh Gilbert, a younger and more energetic man, "a man," says Gorges, " worthy to be beloved of them all for his industry," was forthwith appointed president; and the change was rather a

4

benefit, than otherwise, to the Colony, if anything could benefit what was *in articulo mortis.*

The death of Sir John Popham was a more serious matter. He was the head and front of the enterprise; the brother was only his agent. It was Sir John's Colony. He furnished the bulk of the capital, provided the colonists, gave his name and his own personal infamy to the undertaking. Who, then, was Sir John Popham? He was Lord Chief Justice of England, and was seventy-six years of age. In his youth he had been a highwayman, and probably a garroter. "He frequently sallied forth at night from a hostel in Southwark, with a band of desperate characters, and, planting themselves in ambush on Shooter's Hill, or taking other positions favorable for attack and escape, they stopped travelers and took from them not only their money, but any valuable commodities which they carried with them. The extraordinary and almost incredible circumstance is, that Popham is supposed to have continued in these courses after he had been called to the bar, and when, being of mature age, he was married to a respectable woman." (Lord Campbell's Lives of the Chief Justices, 1849-57, i. p. 210.) Lord Campbell was not the man to speak unadvisedly of one who had occupied the highest judicial office, save one, in England. "Popham's portrait," he says, "represented him as 'a huge, heavy, ugly man,' and I am afraid he would not appear to great advantage in a sketch of his moral qualities, which, lest I should do him injustice I will not attempt." — Idem, p. 229.

With regard to his law reports, Lord Campbell says "they are wretchedly ill done, and they are not considered of authority. We should have been better pleased if he had given us an account of his exploits when he was chief of a band of freebooters." (p. 229.) "The reproach urged against him was extreme severity to prisoners. He was notorious as a 'hanging judge.' Not only was he keen to convict in cases prosecuted by the government; but in ordinary larcenies, and above all in highway

robberies, there was little chance of an acquittal before him."
— Idem. p. 219.

"He left behind him the greatest estate that had ever been
amassed by any lawyer. Some said as much as £10,000 a year;
but it is not supposed to be all honestly come by; and he is
reported even to have begun to save money when 'the road did
him justice.'" — Idem. p. 229.

His other biographers, Fuller, Aubrey, Lloyd, Wood and Foss,
paint his character in similar colors. They allude to, and several
of them state at large, the shocking details of the manner in
which he came into possession of Littlecote Hall, his estate
in Wiltshire, by compounding with felony. Foss, the latest
biographer of the Judges of England, who is disposed to soften
the hard places in Popham's record, mentions this dark story,
and says, (vi. pp. 183–84.) "It is extraordinary that no refu-
tation should have been attempted; for, if any existed, it is to
be presumed that such a writer as Sir Walter Scott, while de-
tailing the charge [in Rokeby] would have noticed the answer."
The "horrible and mysterious crime" alluded to by Macaulay
(Hist. of Eng., ii. p. 542) refers to this affair. Here is the man,
who — the Maine Historical Society would have us believe —
planted civilization on this continent. Let us see how he did it.

His position as Chief Justice gave him a controlling influence
in all the jails and penitentiaries in the realm. Aubrey (Letters,
iii. p. 495) says "he stockt or planted [Northern] Virginia out
of all the gaoles of England." Wood's Athenæ Oxonienses
(Bliss's ed. ii. p. 22) says, "he was the first person who invented
the plan of sending convicts to the plantations." The statement
should have been limited to Englishmen; for the French had
practised this mode of colonization many years before. Cartier
in 1547, La Roche in 1598, and De Montes in 1604, all used
this material for colonists. The permission which the King of
France gave Cartier to ransack the jails of Paris may be found
in Hazard, i. p. 21. Any sort of criminals he could take,

except those convicted of treason, or counterfeiting the King's currency.

Thomas Fuller (Worthies of England, ii. p. 284) says "his [Popham's] justice was exemplary on Theeves and Robbers." Wood quotes this passage, adding, " whose wayes and courses he well understood when he was a young man," and connects it with the fact of his sending convicts to the plantations. Fuller, in his essay on Plantations, in "Holy and Profane States," 1642, says : " If the planters be such as leap thither from the gallows, can any hope for cream out of scum, when men send, as I may say, Christian savages to heathen savages? It is rather bitterly than *falsely* spoken concerning *one* of our Western plantations, consisting of most dissolute people, that it was very like unto England, as being spit out of the very mouth of it." David Lloyd (State Worthies. 1766, ii. p. 46) gives a sketch of Chief Justice Popham, in which, quoting the words of Fuller, already cited, he goes on to say : " neither did he only punish malefactors, but provide for them. He first set up the discovery of New England to maintain and employ those that could not live honestly in the Old." Lloyd also, in this connection, quotes the passage we have cited from Lord Bacon (p. 23), showing that it was understood by the old English historians as applying to the Popham Colony.

The authorities seem to be conclusive as to the character of the colonists sent to Sagadahoc, the person by whom, and the manner in which, they were " prepared ;"— for that is the expression Strachey uses (p. 163) with regard to these very colonists. Popham had sent out the year before (1606) a colony of one hundred persons destined to the same place. The ship was captured by the Spaniards, and the persons taken to Spain, and "made slaves in their gallions." The loss of the ship and outfit was suitably lamented ; but not one word of sympathy was expressed by the old writers for the persons enslaved by the Spaniards ; nor did Popham, so far as we know, make any attempt to rescue them from their hard fate; but he forthwith "prepared a greater number of planters," — that is, the one hundred and twenty persons who afterwards landed at Sabino. If it is pretended that the first company were honest, worthy men, the assumption carries with it the necessary inference that Popham was a heartless wretch; but, assuming that they also were criminals, it was natural that he should leave them to their fate.

The death of Popham, on the 10th of June, 1607,—only eleven days after the Popham colonists sailed [1] — was of course fatal to the original plan of the undertaking. There was no authority left to "prepare" convicts, — colonists, we mean. A criminal colony needs constant recuperation. Seventy-five of the hundred and twenty abandoned the colony before the end of four months. Why they returned to England on the first opportunity that offered, is not recorded. As they were the majority, they probably entered into a conspiracy, and deserted; or they behaved so badly, that the managers were glad to be rid of them, expecting that the Chief Justice would "prepare" others. But his Lordship was dead, though they knew it not; and with him died all hopes of continuing the enterprise. The good ship "Mary and John" returned in the spring with provisions, but with no recruits; and wound up the concern, by taking back to England the managers, and such of the wretched culprits as wished to return.

Perhaps we may as well notice here, as in another place, the only evidence "Sabino" brings forward to show that the Sagadahoc colonists were not convicted criminals, only convicted vagabonds and political offenders. It is this: "Chalmers says there was no transportation of any class of the guilty till 1619. Therefore there was none to Sagadahoc." Chalmers, we beg to submit, is not an original authority. He died only about

---

[1] For the date of Popham's death, we have followed Foss rather than Campbell. The latter fixes the date as June 1, 1607, only one day after the colonists sailed. Campbell has fallen into a mistake in making Popham's age seventy-two; for Campbell himself, and the other authorities, give the date of his birth as 1531.

forty years ago; and our surprise is that "Sabino" should quote him in the face of the old writers. Chalmers had no means of information which writers to-day do not possess, and it seems he did not even use what he had. He was so little acquainted with the history of the Popham Colony as not to know the name of the president who died at Sagadahoc. He gives the name of the person as Gilbert. It is but justice to the name of Chalmers to state that he made no such statement as "Sabino" attributes to him. He says simply that the policy of sending convicts to the plantations originated with King James; and, that in the year 1619, he issued an order to send one hundred dissolute persons to Virginia. There is not an intimation in Chalmers that "there was no transportation of any class of the guilty till 1619."

"Sabino" also finds much consolation "that the law has not been shown requiring transportation as a punishment for moral guilt during the time of the incipiency, continuance and end of the Popham Colony." Will "Sabino" please point out the "law" under which James sent off one hundred convicts in 1619 that did not exist in 1606? It seems never to have occurred to "Sabino," that, under the impulse of avarice, or baser motives, some things can be done without law. There was no statute of the realm requiring John Popham to commit highway robbery, yet he did waylay travelers at night, and relieve them of their purses and other valuables. But there was a law in 1606, (39 Elizabeth, ch. iv.) which, under Popham's construction, was sufficiently ample to cover his plan of colonization. But we must return to the examination of "Sabino's" theory.

6. We confess our inability to understand the concluding clause of "Sabino's" statement. The Popham Colony "was followed by a succession of occupancies that proved title, &c." What occupancies, pray? There was no later occupancy of New England till the Pilgrims arrived in 1620. No genuine Pophamite would, for an instant, admit that the Plymouth Colony had any relation to English supremacy in New England. "Re-

garded as a political event the Pilgrim settlement was not of the slightest consequence or importance." (Mr. John A. Poor's Vindication of Gorges, p. 72). The next event in New England history was the occupancy of Massachusetts Bay. He cannot allude to this. " Puritan " is a more distasteful word to the Maine theorists than " Pilgrim." Besides, Puritan and Pilgrim have no relation to, or connection with, Popham. We are evidently drifting away from the true interpretation, and for the present must remain in blissful ignorance of the full meaning of this Delphic utterance.

The general intent of "Sabino" is not obscure. He would have his readers understand that the Popham affair led to something that was favorable to English supremacy. This we deny, and for proof, again appeal to the record. Can "Sabino" name one of the Popham men that ever took part in, or encouraged, any subsequent settlement? Does he not know that they circulated the most unfavorable reports of the country, and prevented for many years any attempt to occupy New England? Judge Sullivan (History of District of Maine, p. 53) says, "The sufferings of this [Popham] party, and the disagreeable account which they were obliged to give to excuse their own conduct, discouraged any further attempts by the English." Brief Relation, 1622, (in Purchas, iv. p. 1826,) says, "The arrival of these [Popham] people in England was a wonderful discouragement to all the first undertakers, insomuch as there was no more speech of setting any more Plantations in those parts for a long time after." Gorges, (Briefe Narration, p. 10) speaking of the return of the Popham colonists, says, "by which means all our former hopes were frozen to death." Among his misfortunes, which he goes on to enumerate,—for he was a large holder of Popham stock,— was that the country was "wholly given over by the body of the adventurers, as also that it self was branded by the returne of the Plantation as being over cold, and in respect to that, not habitable by our Nation." This statement he must have had from the principal men of the Colony, and shows that they were as destitute of veracity, as the main body of the colonists were wanting in the cardinal virtues enjoined in the Decalogue. Assuming Strachey's account to be correct, we know that the winter of 1607–8, on the coast of Maine, could not have been severe for that locality, whatever the season was in Europe. After the 15th of December. they finished trenching the fort, which shows that there was little or no frost in the ground. The amount of work also performed in the winter would have been absolutely impossible in a severe season. Gorges thus expressed his disbelief in the reports he received, as to the severity of the weather : " I have had too much experience in the World to be frighted with such a blast."

Sir William Alexander, Earl of Stirling. the patentee of Nova Scotia. (Description of New England, 1630, p. 30) thus describes what the Popham Colony did for English supremacy in New England : —

" Thofe that went thither, being preffed to that enterprize, as endangered by the Law, or their own neceffities, (no enforced thing prouing pleafant, difcontented perfons fuffering while they act can feldom haue good fuccefie, and neuer fatiffaction) they after a Winter ftay dreaming of new hopes at home returned backe with the firft occafion, and to iuftify the fuddenneffe of their returne, they did coyne many excufes, burdening the bounds where they had beene with all the afperfions that poffibly they could deuife, feeking by that meanes to difcourage all others."

" Our people abandoning the plantation," says " Brief Relation." (Purchas, iv. p. 1828) " in this sort as you have heard, the Frenchmen immediately took the opportunity to settle themselves within our limits." So far. then, from keeping the Frenchmen out, the Colony invited them in. In the face of such evidence "Sabino" asserts. that the Popham affair " proved title as against the former and never-renewed claims of France." Does he mean that the French claims were never renewed after 1608 ?

Would he wipe out from history the French and Indian wars, and the bloody strife for supremacy between the French and English, that went on for a century and a half, and culminated in the overthrow of French power in 1760?

We have thus with patience, and we trust with candor, examined in detail "Sabino's" statement of the Popham theory; and, if in our former article we slighted its historic claims, they have now, we hope, received due attention.

"Sabino" omitted from his formal statement — but inserted it in another part of his paper — the claim which Popham writers usually bring into the foreground, namely, that the Popham Colony was "the *first* colonial occupation of the soil of New England under English enterprise." What rank will he assign to Bartholomew Gosnold's occupation of Cuttyhunk, on the south shore of Massachusetts, in 1602? Gosnold there and then made a settlement, which he intended to be permanent. He and his men built a fort and a storehouse, and collected a valuable freight to send home to England. The cellar walls of the house they occupied can be identified at the present day. They planted wheat, barley and oats. "Here," says Bancroft, (i. p. 112,) "the foundations of the first New England colony were to be laid." We do not claim that Gosnold founded a colony. He attempted it, and failed; but he did all that the Popham people did, and even more. He made American colonization an honorable enterprise, and showed that it could be made profitable. Gosnold's men were not convicts. They each had a share in the undertaking; and jealousy as to the distribution of their gains led to the return of the whole company to England. The sale of their freight made it a profitable adventure. They spread the most favorable reports of the regions they had visited, and brought the best evidence that it was a country worth possessing. The Popham men, on the other hand, returned to England in penury and disgrace, "burdening the bounds where they had beene with all the aspersions

5

that possibly they could deuise, seeking by that meanes to dis-
courage all others." The death of Queen Elizabeth prevented
Gosnold's return to the Elizabeth Islands; but his representa-
tions and cheerful energy awakened an interest in America that
resulted in the Charter of 1606, under which the Northern and
Southern Virginia settlements were projected. When we com-
pare what Gosnold and his men did in 1602, with what Popham
and his felons did in 1607, it requires a degree of audacity
rising to sublimity to assert, that "the Popham Colony was the
first colonial occupation of the soil of New England under
English enterprise."

Ex-Governor Washburn, of Cambridge, in a speech he made
at the first Popham Celebration in 1862, suggested that if they
would set up the claim that Noah's Ark landed on one of the
adjacent hills, and arrange a Celebration in honor of the event,
he would volunteer to come and take part in it, without doubting
it was true (Pop. Mem., p. 157). The suggestion is worthy of
the serious consideration of the Pophamites. The historical diffi-
culties in the way are but mole-hills compared with the Alpine
absurdities of their present theory. Noah's Ark was an important
fact in the history of the human race. Noah and his family
were respectable persons. The only circumstance we know, to
the discredit of the old patriarch, is excusable on the ground
that there was then no "Maine Law," or even a "judicious
license system." The prejudice attached to the descendants of
one of his sons, has been neutralized by the Emancipation Proc-
lamation, and the passage of the Civil Rights Bill over the head
of President Johnson. The coast is now clear for Noah's Ark.
Let the Celebration come off by all means. Why is it more un-
reasonable to suppose that the Eastern Continent was settled
from the Western, than *vice versa*? Much as we hate celebrations of all kinds, we also volunteer; and, if we cannot attend,
we promise to write a letter, developing still further the theory;
and "Sabino" shall have full permission to print it as an Appendix to the public address.

"Sabino" is evidently in trouble about the "cannon story," and well he may be. He says "Williamson is inclined to discredit it." Williamson has this inclination, not on the ground of lack of evidence that it occurred; but on the ground of its shocking inhumanity, and the discredit it throws upon the colonists. We are inclined to discredit it, because of the disgrace it casts upon the human race. But the ugly fact still remains (to use Williamson's words) that it was "believed to be true by the ancient and well-informed inhabitants on the Sagadahoc." Again "Sabino" would have us believe, that, whereas the Indians, several years later, told the Jesuit missionaries some of the outrages they had suffered from the Popham colonists, and did not tell them this, therefore the story was invented in Massachusetts, seventy years after it was alleged to have happened. The Jesuits, in their Relations, were describing the friendly feelings of the Indians towards themselves. They doubtless heard, with the other cruelties mentioned, the cannon story; but they rightly judged, that, while it would not contribute to the point they were illustrating, it would appear to readers so inhuman, and hence so improbable, as to weaken the credibility of their other statements. Besides, "Sabino's" argument founded on an omission, if it proves anything, proves too much for him. It proves that not one of the many propositions set up by the Pophamites are true, for not one of them is mentioned in the Jesuit Relations. The insinuation that the cannon story originated in Massachusetts, is a curious and comical blunder. The District of Maine, Fort Popham included, was at the date specified a part of Massachusetts. "Sabino" sees this foot-note in Williamson: "Supplement to King Philip's Wars, A. D., 1675, p. 75," and he supposes that 1675 was the date the statement was published, whereas it was the date when King Philip's War commenced. The book was not printed till 1716. He does not inform us how "the ancient and well-informed inhabitants on the Sagadahoc" could have been misled by a statement invented in Massachusetts in 1716.

"Sabino" firmly holds, with Mr. Kidder, that the vessel of thirty tons, built at Sagadahoc, made a voyage across the ocean. "Brief Relation, 1622," he says, "gives us much information about its arrival in England as about the arrival of the ship." But "Brief Relation" says nothing about the arrival of either vessel. It records simply, "the arrival of *these people* here in England was a wonderful discouragement," etc. The leaders, and the main body of these people, we believe, returned safely to England in the "Mary and John;" and this is sufficient to fulfil all the conditions of the narrative in "Briefe Narration," Strachey and the other old chroniclers. "Sabino," however, is ambitious that all (including those who left in the "pretty pynnace") should arrive in England, and show up the new craft. He says, "This word *all* used by Gorges and Ogilby utterly forbids the statement of your correspondent." Gorges's *all* has no reference to the arrival in England. His words are, "all resolved to quit the place (Sagadahoc) and with one consent to away." That "Sabino" should quote Ogilby as an authority, indicates an unfamiliarity in the authentic sources of New England history which we regret to see. Mr. John A. Poor (Popham Memorial, p. 73) says: "It is well known that the Popham Colony, *or a portion of them*, returned to England in 1608." It strengthens Mr. Poor's argument on the importance of the Colony in maintaining English supremacy, to claim that a portion of the colonists remained in the country. We have quoted the opinion of our esteemed Portland friend for "Sabino's" benefit; and not because it carries additional conviction to our mind. One who writes after this fashion: "They finished their vessel of fifty (?) tons in the winter and spring, called the Virginia, of Sagadahoc, in which they returned to England,"—thus adding twenty tons to the size of the vessel, and crowding all into the "pretty pynnace," leaving the "Mary and John" to return in ballast,—is not amenable to the common code of literary and historical criticism.

The Popham Colony, in fine, was a scandalous and complete failure. The thing, as an historical event, was dead and buried. The grass, for more than two centuries and a half, had kindly grown over it, obliterating even from the memory of man the spot where those disgraceful scenes were enacted. In the year 1849, the Hakluyt Society of London printed Strachey's narration, and furnished a clew to the burial place. Nothing would satisfy a few excellent people in Maine but to dig up the sickening remains, and flaunt them under the nostrils of the community. Here was an offense against decency and sanitary regulations, indictable at common law. In cholera times the proceeding is insufferable.

No one imagines that the Popham investigators commenced operations with any other than the amiable motive of contributing to the historic glories of their native State. But they knew not for what they were digging. Their first mistake was, that, when they came to the putrid mass, they did not carefully replace the sod, and say nothing about it. Instead of this, every man shouted "Eureka!" They arranged a monster gathering, and invited all creation to celebrate with them the Two-hundred and Fiftieth Popham Anniversary. People came from the ends of the earth; enjoyed a generous Eastern hospitality; "drank water, if not inspiration, out of the existent Popham well" (Query — Is "Sabino" quite sure that the inspiration came from the *well*?), believed as much as they could, and had a good time generally. Perhaps history manufactured in this way will stand; but we think not.

Because historical writers have presumed to examine and question their theory, they have grown sullen and morose. They abuse Massachusetts; they spit at Plymouth Rock; they berate the Puritans; they eulogize Sir John Popham; and they sigh for a system of mediaeval barbarism which Popham and Gorges could not plant on New England soil, because God, in his mercy to the human race, had decreed otherwise.

The true historic glory of the noble State of Maine seems to
have been lost sight of, in the antiquarian researches of her
zealous sons, — which is, that the State sprang from the loins of
Massachusetts. To this fact, the State to-day is indebted for
every one of those distinctive elements of general intelligence,
enterprise and thrift that make her what she is, — a New England State, instead of a feudal Virginia or a South Carolina.
The Massachusetts Puritans came in early, and took possession
of the land, under a technical construction they gave to their
own charter, organized municipalities, set up their churches and
schools, and put down with a strong hand all opposition to their
authority. The historian of New Hampshire has given a faithful
picture of the social condition of the Gorges plantation on the
Agamenticus (York) River, when the Puritans commenced their
missionary operations.

"The people were without order or morals, and it is said of
some of them, that they had as many shares in a woman, as they
had in a fishing-boat. . . . . No provision was made for public
institutions, schools were unknown, and they had no ministers,
till, in pity of their deplorable state, two went thither from Boston
on a voluntary mission." Belknap's American Biography, i. p.
387-8. See also Hutchinson's Collections, p. 424.

The appearance of the Puritans among them did not to the
Gorges men seem joyous, but grievous; nevertheless afterward
it yielded the peaceable fruit of civilization and godliness unto
them who were exercised thereby. The territory was thus saved
from the ethics of Popham, the prelacy of Laud and the Stuarts,
and the barbarism of a colony of outlaws. The civilization of
the District of Maine, during the colonial period, was as essen-
tially Puritan, as that of Massachusetts Bay; and the District
was represented in the General Court at Boston, from the year
1653. This close political and social union continued till the
admission of the State into the Union in 1820.

It is the privilege, therefore, of the historical writers of Maine, to turn from the unpleasant topic that of late has engaged their attention, to the more congenial theme we have suggested. Let them, with filial affection, recount the virtues and deeds of their Puritan ancestors; and, if they must have an event to celebrate, let it be the landing on Plymouth Rock in 1620, or the arrival of Winthrop and the Charter in 1630, — events which are theirs to celebrate, as well as ours. P.

P.S. — We ought perhaps to acknowledge Mr. Kidder's kindness in sending to us a corrected copy of his article in the Portland Advertiser, in reply to our notice of Prof. Patterson's Address. The article still has so many literary and historical errors, that it would be unkindness to its author to review it in its present condition. We can imagine the inconvenience of having one's writings printed so far from home. If Mr. Kidder will furnish us with another copy, still further revised, we promise to give it all the attention it deserves. P.

[*Boston Daily Advertiser, July 28, 1866.*]

THE POPHAM COLONY, " FINALLY."

To the Editors of the Boston Daily Advertiser: —

Absences have prevented my notice of the article of your correspondent "P.," as early as I could have wished. I now take it up for some remarks on its most prominent positions.

To his criticisms, both merited and unmerited, I desire to bow in meek thankfulness. They are merited only as the imperfections were the result of haste in writing on the eve of a journey. Though they may injure the advocate, the cause stands as impregnable as ever. The unmerited are to be attributed to the indistinctness of my rapid penmanship. If our articles shall have the fortune to come to a second edition, he will not be sorry to see that his sagacity has been made useful in aid of my argument.

As to the pervading personalities in the communication, I have
but little to say. Of my position and acts in connection with
the commemorations of the colony, it asserts matters which
never existed, and attributes to me motives which I have never
entertained. These allegations do not change the facts of
history. It is because of this *personal* phase of the discussion,
that I propose to make no farther reply to your correspondent,
even if he should attempt a sur-rejoinder. I do not know him.
But he seems to know me, in this connection, more than well, —
more than I know of myself, or any one knows or can know
of me.

In ascribing to me the origination of the celebrations of the
Popham Colony, the communication ignores the fact, that the
"founding" thereof (and I use the word in its dictionary sense)
was commemorated, in "a bi-centenary celebration," by the Rev.
Dr. Jenks, "with a party of gentlemen, in 1807." So that, if
there could be claimed any virtue for an Episcopal origination
of the commemorative visit to Sabino, — which has never been
claimed by any one acquainted with the facts, — this early act
by this lover of the olden days would take it all away. Indeed,
I have had nothing to do with the later celebrations, as their
"original inventor and patentee," in any sense whatever. Its
suggestion even was not Episcopal, but simply historical. I
have been only auxiliary.

The communication has not a little to say about the bad traits
of character in Chief Justice Popham, as displayed in a portion
of his early manhood. But it wholly neglects testimony —
elsewhere cited — to traits of an opposite kind, appearing in his
more matured years. This evidence appears in the writings of
his cotemporaries, who speak of him in terms of high commendation. Whatever might have been his earlier life, the path of
repentance and amendment was open for his entrance. After
his marriage, he changed his early courses; and by his diligence
in his legal studies qualified himself for his later eminent posi-

tion. When Strachey, Smith, Croke and Mather, writing after
his death, and of course after his character was completed, call
him "the upright and noble gentleman," "that honorable pattern
of virtue," "a person of great learning and integrity," "the
noble lord," with other words of approval, and none of censure,
a reader of the paper cannot but wonder that the better part
of his later life was not noticed as well as the worse parts of
his earlier. Fuller has placed him among the "Worthies," and
says: "If *Quicksilver* could really be *fixed*, to what a treasure
would it amount! Such is *wild youth* seriously reduced to
gravity, as by this young man did appear."

The opinion of Lord Campbell in his favor should not be
neglected by an impartial seeker for truth. He is severe on
most of the Chief Justices, not sparing even the good Sir Matthew
Hale. His commendations are therefore the more valuable. In
his "Life" of this Chief Justice, he describes the particular traits
to his discredit, when, with other young men, he entered on his
illegal acts on the highway; and then says, "We must remember
that this calling was not then so discreditable as it became afterwards." He speaks of the change in his purposes; his diligence
as a student; and, after some quotations presented in this discussion, he says, "He held the office (of Chief Justice) fifteen
years, and was supposed to conduct himself in it very credit-
ably." "Many of his judgments in civil cases are preserved,
showing that he well deserved the reputation which he enjoyed."
"On the trial of actions between party and party, he is allowed
to be strictly impartial, and to have expounded the law clearly
and soundly." "I believe that no charge could justly be made
against his purity as a judge."

And then, as to the reasons why censures were brought against
him, this biographer says, "Yet, from the recollection of his
early history, some suspicion always hung about him, and
stories, probably quite groundless, were circulated to his disad-
vantage." "Of these we have a specimen" about "Littlecote

6

Hall." It is "unfair to load the memory of a judge with the
obloquy of so great a crime, upon such unsatisfactory testimony."
A distinguished ruler — more exalted than Popham, whom Pal-
frey calls " that eminent person "— once wrote, " Remember not
the sins of my youth."

If he was called "the hanging judge," it was because criminals
were to be punished. Lloyd says, to his credit, that "the deserved death of some scores preserved the lives and livelihood
of some thousands; travellers owing their safety to this judge's
severity many years after his death." Aubrey says the same.

But, if all were true, as alleged to the disparagement of the
Chief Justice, is there so necessary a connection between him and
the colonists at Sabino as that they, except the ten men in office,
must therefore have been "villains and convicts"? He certainly
has on all sides the praise of having been the earliest and the
most active promoter of colonization on our wild New England
shores. In this relation he gained the distinct commendation of
Hubbard, as " the first that ever procured men or means to
possess New England,"—" the main pillar " of the enterprise,
with not the remotest allusion to any such acts in its accomplish-
ment as are mentioned by your correspondent. His statement
leads one to think, that he regarded these early movements as
preparatory to the settlements in Massachusetts. He certainly
has said nothing that can lead us to suppose he connected
"convicts" with Popham's efforts.

There is a statement made, derived from Strachey's use of the
word "prepared," in two instances, as though this *preparation*
consisted chiefly in furnishing convicts for transportation to Sagadahoc. Where is the proof? There is not a word in the con-
text to warrant any such application, and indeed no where else.
One of the " prepared " expeditions was captured by a Spanish
fleet, and the men held in a kind of piratical duress. The communication proceeds to say, in condemnation of the old historians
and Popham, that "no word of sympathy was expressed by the

old writers for the persons enslaved by the Spaniards; nor did Popham, so far as we know, make any attempts to rescue them from their hard fate." Alas! where is the proof of this sweeping assertion? Exactly opposite was the fact. His humane regard for the captives was forthwith put into action. It would have been well for the furtherance of history, if one well versed in "the old writers" against Popham had also seen and produced a single testimony in his favor. Take one sentence from Gorges, relating to this Spanish capture : "The affliction of the captain and his company put the Lord Chief Justice to charge and myself to trouble in procuring their liberties, which was not soon obtained." This citation is enough to show his efforts for their release, and proves great humanity on the part of this "noble patron of justice and virtue," as he has been well described; and that he was not herein "a heartless wretch," as your correspondent writes, and furnishes no proof of his allegation.

The quotations from Lloyd — himself mostly valuable for *his* quotations — are prominently presented, as bearing on the character of the colonists. He says that Popham "provided for malefactors." But that is no certain proof that he sent them to Sagadahoc. The plan and its completion are different things, and its completion was not necessarily here. "He first set up the discovery of New England to maintain and employ those that could not honestly live in the Old." But this proposal, this "setting up," if made in regard to Sagadahoc, does not *prove* that the suggestion was ever carried out. With the singularly imperfect knowledge of foreign geography, that has always characterized English education, all Virginia seems to have been New England, and *vice versa*. New England was North and South Virginia. We admit the plan. We demand the proof that convicts were banished to this region. Besides, where is the inhumanity of the proposal, or its fulfilment? It was intended to save the lives of criminals, who otherwise would have been hung, according to evidence and the laws of their time ;

and doubtless the culprits condemned would have deemed the provision merciful, that by banishment allowed them to live.

The quotation from Sir William Alexander has been often made; and it is valuable, as coinciding accurately with the views expressed in my communications. His book is rare; and I take his words from your columns: —

"Thofe that went thither being preffed to that enterprize, as endangered by the Law, or their own neceffities, (no enforced thing prouing pleafant, difcontented perfons fuffering while they act can feldom have good fuccefs and neuer fatiffaction) they after a Winter flay dreaming of new hopes at home returned back with the firft occafion."

Here we are accurately taught that the people — that is, the laborers in the colony — went "as endangered by the law, or their own necessities." How were they "endangered"? By what "law"? By what "necessity"? A writer of that time furnishes the reply, — in the crowded population, the poverty of the working class, and the encroachments of their rich neighbors; and urges emigration as the relief. He writes the following: —

"Look seriously into the land, and see whether there bee not just cause, if not a necessity to seek abroad. The people do swarme in the land as young bees in a hive in June: insomuch that there is hardly room for one man to live by another. The mightier, like old strong bees, thrust the weaker, as younger out of their hives. Lords of manors convert townships, in which were a hundredth or two hundredth communicants, to a shepheard and his dog. The true laboring husbandman, that sustaineth the prince by the plow, who was wont to feed many poore, to set many people on work, and pay twice as much subsidie and fifteenes to the king for his proportion of earth, as his landlord did for ten times as much; that was wont to furnish the church with saints, the musters with able persons to fight for their soveraigne, is now turned laborer, and can hardly scape the statutes of rogues and vagrants. . . . The poore

metall man worketh his bones out and swelteth himself in the fire ;
yet for all his labor, having charge of wife and children, he can
hardly keep himselfe from the almes box. . . . The poor man
receiveth very neere four pence for every sixepeny worth of work.
The thoughtfull poore woman that hath her small children standing
at her side and hanging on her breast, she worketh with her needle
and laboureth with her fingers, her candle goeth not out by night,
she is often deluding the bitterness of her life with sweete songs, that
she singeth to a heavy heart. . . . I warrant you her songs want
no passion ; she never saith, O Lord, but a salt teare droppeth
from her sorrowfull heart, that weepeth with the head for company
with teares of sweetest bloud. And when all the week is ended,
she can hardly earn salt enough for her water gruel to feede on
upon the Sunday."

Surely here is a picture of extreme poverty, — fully corrobo-
rated by a document in Mather, — showing how "the land grew
weary of her inhabitants;" and how "children, neighbors and
friends, especially the poor, were counted the greatest bur-
dens." It tells us how the honest yeomanry and worthy laborers of that day were harassed by the encroachments of their
"mightier" neighbors, and the rigid oppression of the civil law.
They were "endangered" through no fault of their own. One
cannot but recall a part of the petition of Agur, — "lest I be
poor, and steal" to support life. But are we to consider such
men as "rascals and villains"? And were any such men, sentenced, as men of guilt, to go forth as a part of the colony?
Symonds here gives a full and sufficient interpretation to the
meaning of Lloyd and Alexander.

Let us now see who had the power to sentence and fix the
place of exile. The Statute of 39 Elizabeth c. iv, 1597-8,
to which your correspondent refers as being ample enough to
cover "the plan of colonizing by banishment of convicts," au-
thorizes this penalty for "dangerous rogues," who "shall and
may lawfully be banished out of this Realme and all other the
Domynious thereof." This was to be done "by the Justices of

the Peace" at the "Quarter Sessions." Not a word is said
about the Chief Justice. The place to which they were to be
sent was to be decided "by the Privic Council;" and thus, certainly, not by Popham alone. So that, if there were shame in the
transaction, the most honored men of the nation were equally
involved in the disgrace. It is unfair and ungenerous to single
him out to meet a purpose, as the sole object of obloquy and
rebuke.

And now, as to the return of these persons to England. Your
correspondent, assuming that a part of them were convicts, truly
says, in agreement with his assumption, that they would not be
"over-anxious to revisit their native land. They had saved
their necks once by emigrating, and were not in haste to put
them again into the halter." And so he invents the story about
a second pinnace, with which they could "lead generally a wild
and free life, such as was congenial to their character and dispositions." This is a precious statement; but it happens to be
directly opposite to the citation fearlessly made from Sir William
Alexander, which declares that "Those that went thither, — as
endangered by the laws, — dreaming of new hopes of home, returned thither with the first occasion." None were left behind.
If they had been convicts, they would have pursued some such
plan as is intimated by your correspondent, and not have gone
back to the hazard of certain death. For the statute last quoted
enacts, "if any such Rogues, so banished as aforesaid, shall
returne againe into any part of this Realme or Dominion of
Wales without lawful Lycence or Warrant so to do, that in
every such case such offence shall be Fellony, and the Party
offending therein shall suffer Death as in case of Fellony." This
was but poor encouragement for convicts to seek their native
shores. The winter had been hard. But Captain Davies, who
had borne news of the "success" of the enterprise to England,
had come back to Sagadahoc in the spring, "with a shipp laden
full of vitualls" and other useful things, so that starvation had

no horrors; and the summer was at hand. Sir William testifies that they had "new hopes" inviting them to go home. But, if they were condemned criminals, what "new hopes" could have been cherished by men who had nothing to expect but certain detection, by the letter R "branded in the left shoulder," for identification, as soon as they stepped on their native shores; and penal death as its sequel? These "hopes" must have been "new" indeed, if they rested only on a halter, a hangman, and a gallows! Here your correspondent and one of his chief witnesses entirely disagree. The former says, they "were not over-anxious to revisit their native land," fearing the halter. The witness says, that "they returned back with the first occasion"— hasting, and hopeful of a better condition than the one they had left. The one says, that, as liberated jail-birds, they led a roving life here, fearing death at home. The other, in effect, says they had a happy voyage to England, with bright anticipations of a more prosperous life!

We may now look at the kind of men who were to go as settlers to the early colonies on our coast. The Charter of James, April 10, 1606, under which this colony was formed, gives the information. It proves that the specially enumerated patentees, "they and every one of them, shall and may, at all and every time and times hereafter, have, take, and lead in the said voyage, and for and towards the said Plantations, and Colonies, and to travel thitherward, and to abide and inhabit there, in every the said Colonies and plantations, such and so many of our subjects as shall willingly accompany them or any of them, in the said voyages and Plantations."

The reader will note the sole condition annexed, as to the persons selected to go: "such and so many of our subjects, as shall WILLINGLY accompany" any or all of the patentees. Can any language be plainer? Force by the sentence of the civil law is not here thought of. The "willingness" of the "honest," hard pressed yeomanry, seeking to better their livelihood, is here provided for. The " willing " ones are allowed to go, except such as, by the royal power might " be specially restrained." So that the real rogues, however " willing " to go, might thus be forbidden, lest they should contaminate the honest men, described by Gorges, who, " not liking to be hired out as servants to foreign states, thought it better became them to put in practice the reviving resolution of those free spirits, that rather chose to spend themselves in seeking a new world, than servilely to be hired out but as slaughterers in the quarrels of strangers." The same provision existed in the patents to Gilbert and Raleigh. Yet no one has supposed that these leaders took convicts.

Yet this is not all. The same Charter of 1606 expressly provides: " that all and every the Persons being our subjects, which shall dwell and inhabit within every or any of the said several Colonies or Plantations, and every of their Children, which shall happen to be born within any of the Limits and Precincts of the said several Colonies and Plantations, shall HAVE and enjoy all Liberties, Franchises and Immunities, within any of our other Dominions, to all Intents and Purposes, as if they had been abiding and born, within this our Realm of *England*, or any other of our said Dominions." Now, if the Popham Colony was composed of convicts, how enviable their condition! The sentence of the law did not touch them, except in words! They still had all the " Liberties " of the most innocent Englishman on his native soil! They were " subjects," — " loving subjects," as the same class of " willing " emigrants were called in the Charter of 1609. What " convicts " ever had such " Franchises and Immunities " since the world began? Their state was nothing less than perfect freedom! They were, therefore, *no convicts at all;* and so could return home safely, and with " new hopes," just as soon as they deemed the change desirable.

In double confirmation of this fact, we may go to the Charter of 18 James, Nov. 3, 1620, which speaks of the efforts made in divers years past, in the Northern Colony, by former grantees,

who had " taken actual possession of the Continent," and had
" settled already some of our People in Places agreeable to their
Desires in those parts." This, certainly, is very far from sus-
taining the opinion, that the occupants of Sagadahoc were convicts. For they were settled in a place "agreeable to their
Desires," until calamities darkened all their prospects. It is
worth noting here, that Lord Campbell says nothing about Popham in connection with convicts and the colony. This omission
is significant.

A question is proposed, with an air of confidence, as if its
answer must demolish the positions of my former article. It is
this : " Will ·Sabino' please point out the ' law ' under which
James sent off a hundred convicts in 1619, that did not exist in
1606 ?" The demand is adroitly made, but not pertinently.
To make it touch the point, it should have been 1607. My reply
is readily given.

The statute for the punishment of rogues by banishment, already noted. (39 Eliz. ch. iv.,) expired by its own limitation, in
1601 ; when it was renewed, to continue till the end of the first session of the next Parliament, which was held in 1603–4. It was
then re-enacted, (1 James. ch. iv. and xxv.,) when the additional
provision was made, that persons condemned under its sanctions
should be branded on the left shoulder with "a greate Romane
R," for their detection in case of their unlicensed return, so as to
secure the death of the offender, "as in case of Felonie." This
statute was to continue "until the end of the first session of the
next Parliament" (ch. xxv.). I have no means at hand of knowing the precise date when this session closed ; but the Parliament itself ended on May 27. 1606, and the *statute was not
revived*. The temper of the king and that body was shown in
the statute (3 James ch. xxvii.) entitled, "An acte for the King's
most gracious generall and free Pardon." The next Parliament
began Nov. 18. 1606, and ended July 4, 1607. Such was
the forbearance of the supreme legislature in relation to the

7

transportation of condemned criminals, that the session passed away, and the law, that had expired by its own limitation, was allowed to remain in this state of its natural death. Transportation seems not to have been in favor.

Therefore, from "the end of the firste session" of the Parliament whose final session was terminated May 27, 1606, till, after the Popham Colony sailed, May 31, 1607, there was no statute of transportation in existence.

A re-enactment of the law, or rather a law for punishing rogues by the workhouse, and not by transportation, was not made until the Parliament beginning Feb. 9, 1609. This was four days more than a year after George Popham's death, and a year and a half after the death of the Chief Justice. So that here was at least an interval of more than two years and three-fourths, when there was no law for the exile of convicts from the royal dominions. In this space of time, the Popham Colony had its beginning, its continuance and its end,—beginning more than a year after the law had died; continuing through the larger part of the year; and ending nearly another year before it was revived, in a very different form, and with a milder penalty. During this period, no law appears in the "Statutes of the Realm" for the transportation of convicts; and it is perfectly incredible that any persons were so sentenced by the justices of the peace, and sent to Sagadahoc under any sanction of the highest judicial authority in the realm, with the specific designation of the place by the Privy Council.

The preamble of the statute of 1609 for "punishing rogues" makes known the inactivity of the magistrates in the enforcement of former provisions, and the desuetude into which this law had fallen. It declares that the earlier "Statutes had not been duly and severely putt in execution." Therefore the requisitions are made stronger, to bind the proper officers to their more stringent execution, in regard to "Houses of Correction." Transportation is not even hinted at. This previous easy state of affairs

on this topic shows that the rigor of expulsion, ascribed to Popham, is a thought of later times.

It is also to be noted, that the Charter of 1606 is in strict harmony with the fact that the expired law had not been revived.
Among the twenty-seven Acts of 3, 4 James, 1605–6, and the
thirteen of 4, 5 James, 1606–7, no one appears on the pages to
authorize the exportation of criminals. Those who went to either
of the Virginias were to go "willingly," and enjoy their "liberties." If, in any other book of laws besides the "Statutes of the
Realm," if there be such, or by any new and singular interpretation of any provision there can be found a rule requiring the
transportation of convicts, it will not thence follow that any
were sent to Sagadahoc. For the Charter will still say that only
volunteers were to go, who should be free men as long as they
remained in connection with the company.

I did not refer to Ogilby and Chalmers as original authorities,
but as good investigators. The former has been long known.
My favorable opinion of the latter is drawn from the Preface
to his "Introduction to the History of the Revolt in the American Colonies." Your correspondent seems to undervalue him.
But to sustain my estimate, I may quote the expressions of the
American editor of the above-named volumes. "His works are
deemed to possess much merit as the result of profound research
and a discriminating judgment."—"His official station gave him
access to all state papers."—"He took advantage of this opportunity, to investigate in its original sources the history of the
colonies." — "His work (Political Annals) has ever been
quoted with entire confidence and respect; and this circumstance
speaks clearly in favor of the author's candor and honesty."
When he speaks of no earlier transportation than 1619, I have
been ready to give him credit. Your correspondent refers to
him as writing, " that the policy of sending convicts to the plantations originated with King James, and that in the year 1619
he issued an order to send a hundred dissolute persons to

Virginia." I am content with this statement. Bancroft thinks "some of them were convicts: but it must be remembered that the crimes of which they were convicted were chiefly political:" and political felons, as well as those whom in the same volume he calls "the Puritan felons that freighted the fleet of Winthrop," were "endangered by the law:" and yet not for this reason to be regarded as tainted in the least with moral guilt. His opinion, too, is that there was never sent to South Virginia — for he seems not to have heard of the accusations brought against the northern colony — any "considerable number" of persons convicted of "social crimes:" "certainly not enough to affect its character." This statement may be taken as a sufficient reply to the charge that Popham "stockt" the plantations out of "all the gaoles of England." Indeed, all that Bacon, nearly twenty years after his colony had ceased, and other far later writers have said, on the topic contained in the quotation from him, relates to the later affairs in the southern colony; and can be connected with Popham only as he was a prime mover in the enterprise of colonization, carried on after his death. It cannot be shown that they had Sagadahoc in mind. Weber, as "revised and corrected" by Professor Bowen, adheres to 1619.

Against a remark of mine, the communication states, that there was "no later occupancy of New England till the Pilgrims arrived in 1620." I said "the Popham Colony was followed by a succession of occupancies, that proved title." I say so still. I did not mean that all these occupancies were colonies. They were at Monhegan, by Sir Francis Popham and Captain John Smith; at Pemaquid, by the annual visits of the English from Virginia; at Mount Desert, by Argall; at Saco, by Vines; at Plymouth, by the Pilgrims and by numerous others, after that great and memorable event in our national history. They were made under the protection of the Charter of James in 1606; energetically promoted in the outset by Popham, "the first to procure men and means to possess New England:" and sustained for years at great expense by Sir Ferdinando Gorges. In this connection I wish to supply an omission noticed by your correspondent. where I said, that the colony "proved title as against the former and never-revived claims of France." "West of the Kennebec" was in my mind, but not written. I thank him for the correction, as it strengthens my position. It would have been better to have said, "the French never had any possession on the coast, west of the Kennebec."

As to the settlement of Gosnold, I have before shown that it was not a "chartered colony." It was deserted on the day when its small house was scarcely fitted for a permanent dwelling. It was "undertaken on private account;" asserted no general claim; proved no title; and was not renewed.

The powder and cannon stories appear to be singularly confused by Williamson. His misplaced footnote referring to the History of King Philip's War has misled us both. It is made as authority for the latter, when it should be for the former, and the tradition (I quote from memory) is from "an ancient mariner." As it is unsupported, it can hardly be claimed as history. As to the cannon story, one of our best antiquarians thinks that it has had no earlier mention than is found in Morse and Parish, about two centuries after its alleged occurrence, as derived from the Norridgewock Indians. Such a tradition is of very little account. If these stories had been true, it is marvellous that the "speechifying" Indians round about Arrowsic should not have told their prowess and their sufferings to the listening Jesuits in 1611. It may be well to know that a valued New Hampshire historian locates the narrative about the cannon at Dover, N. H., in the time of Waldron, when a large number of Indians were captured by stratagem. If the servants of the colony set dogs on the meddlesome Indians, the wise men in council in a later colony in New England, as Hazard gives it, decided to employ "mastiffe-dogs" to hunt down Indians in 1656. Why not blame both?

That portions of the population in Maine were corrupt, after settlements were dotted along the coast, is true. Deterioration often follows colonization. For all the influence for good that Massachusetts has spread, here and elsewhere, all ought to be glad, though here it was somewhat irregularly introduced. The celebrations at Sabino Head are not intended to detract from the merits of Plymouth Rock. They were many. It is no harm to wish that they had been more.

The letter of Mr. Kidder relative to the "pretty pynnace of about thirty tonne," is again referred to by your correspondent. What are we to understand by the few notices of her history? Simply this, that on "August 28," "the carpenters labored about the building of a small pinnace." Their first act was to prepare the timber from the surrounding forest,—not necessarily of "green pine," where the ridge bears oak, maple and spruce now, and perhaps did then, — and put it into shape for future use. It was left to season during the autumnal months. Then, after Captain Davies returned to England, with an account of the "forwardness of their plantation," on the 15th of December, the seasoned timber was "framed," and the craft completed, as the "Brief Relation" says, "notwithstanding the coldness of the season and the small help they had." For reasons satisfactory to the leaders of the colony, after Captain Davies returned to them, Strachey says "they all ymbarqued in the new arrived shipp and in the new pynnace, the Virginia, and sett saile for England." Gorges says they "all resolved to quit the place, and with one consent to [go] away." Sir William Alexander says, "Those that went thither . . . returned back with new hopes." The "Briefe Relation" says the news from home "made the whole company to resolve upon nothing but their return with their ships; . . . having built a pretty bark of their own, which served them to good purpose, as easing them in their returning;" and asserts "the arrival of these people here in England,"—of course, the same "people" who embarked, and in the same "ships" in which they commenced the voyage. Any other interpretation will be a violent perversion of language. As to any persons of the colony remaining to be rovers on the coast in another supposed pinnace, it will be time enough to consider that conjecture, when proof shall be brought to change it into history. It will be "credulity" to answer such a "demand" on our faith, as long as it is unsupported by evidence; and we shall still believe that "The Virginia" was not, perhaps the first craft of the Northmen, French, Basques, Dutch, or Indians, of whom we were not thinking — but was the pioneer ship of the *English people* in the new world, and was a striking proof of the skill and enterprise of the laboring colonists, with Digby, the London shipwright, as their head in her construction.

But, whatever may be said of the enterprise or its details, whether favorable or unfavorable, the true and single point for grave consideration is the prominent fact, that a colony was founded at the mouth of the Kennebec under the charter of James, 1606, which Popham "certainly was a chief instrument in procuring," and that this was the *first* thus laid in New England under English sway.

No personalities, no imputation of sinister and never existing motives, no disparagement of the character of the prime movers and later advocates, — for Gorges has been blamed as well as Popham, — no reproaches thrown upon the laboring colonists, and no finger of derision pointed at the failure of their purpose, should turn the reader of history away from this path. The leading minds in England, with the King as their friend, were actuated by the desire to turn to good account the discoveries of the early navigators; the reports of fishermen returning from our coast, and the more systematic researches of Gosnold, who, Strachey says, came "for discovery;" and Weymouth, whose narrative, and Pring, whose exact description pointed out the Kennebec as the place for speedy occupation. Emphasis was given to the determination of the associates, by their bearing with them a charter and a constituent code of laws, carrying out the principles of the English Constitution. An expedition of that nature, and at that time, required relatively much more of thought, energy and means than one of ten times its numbers and power would do at the present day. The fact, that it came directly to the Kennebec, shows that its course and destination did not depend on any capricious views of its commander; but were in accordance with a previously matured plan " for the seizing such a place as they were directed unto by the council of the colony." Its approach near to the claimed territory of France implies a previous knowledge of the coast, and a purpose to take possession within the chartered limits, fully up the undisputed boundary line. This occupation, and those made in the few following years, were called in the patent of 18 James, Nov. 3, 1620, the " actual possession of the continent;" thus showing how exalted a value was placed on these incipient, though feeble measures, by the highest authority in the mother land. The commercial purposes of the undertaking at Sagadahoc were not all. A religious purpose was connected therewith, and carried on during its continuance. Its great purpose was to secure title within the territory granted to the company. Signal disasters attended the later part of its life ; and, though it failed commercially, Gorges " had no reason greatly to despair of means." In its historic influence, and in its opening the way for immediate and successive efforts, it was, in the words of Maine's most worthy and distinguished living historian, " *one* of the steps in the grand march of civilization."

As such, and as the *first* chartered " step " on our rock-bound coast by " English hearts and hands," we have thought it proper to do it honor ; and this too as persons united in no one single denomination of Christians. We have taken pleasure in aiding to bring before the appreciative mind of the community " this *initial point* in the history of the settlement of New England," and its bearing on subsequent settlements along our shores. We

Bishop Burgess, had designed to write at length on this debated subject. He had been in correspondence with the present Duke of Somerset for information on one part of its history. He had already said, and patriotically too, of the chaplain of the colony, "Seymour was the first preacher of the Gospel in the English tongue, within the borders of New England, and of the free, loyal and unrevolted portion of these United States. Had he inherited all the honors of his almost royal grandsire, they would have given him a far less noble place than this, in the history of mankind." But the fatal illness of this eminent historical scholar has prevented the intended gift of his deliberate and final testimony in defence of the claims here set forth in behalf of "that northerne colony uppon the Sagadahoc." SABINO.

[*Boston Daily Advertiser, July 28, 1866.*]

A RUNNING REVIEW OF THE "POPHAM AGAIN AND FINALLY."

To the Editors of the Boston Daily Advertiser: —

By referring to the Supplement of the *Daily Advertiser* of the 31st of May, I see that "pool" has again overflowed, and the result is a wishy-washy everlasting flood of nearly four columns in small type, some of which seem to be a reply to the fairly-written statements and comments of "Sabino;" but the most of it reads very much like one of Van Buren's old messages with which we were served annually, some twenty-five years ago, while in barefaced effrontery it much resembles the speeches of Jeff. Davis and Wigfall, at the commencement of the late rebellion. Let us wade through this mass of matter which reaches from the voyage of Noah to the latest raid on the Pophamites; and here let me remark, that the writer handles that ancient

navigator's character very much as he does Chief Justice Popham's, looking only at its worst side. Why does he not
assert that his ark was built of "green pine," and no one would
embark in it, or, if they did, they went a fishing, and never
arrived at Mount Ararat; for there is just as much evidence of
this as there is in his assertions relative to the vessel built at
Sabino. But let us follow the writer, and see how he replies
to "Sabino." First, he finds great difficulty in understanding
what all others clearly appreciate, and this accounts for many
of his misstatements, for if a man cannot understand the truth,
how can he communicate it? Secondly, he gives us a short
lesson on style; but finally concludes "that, after all, it is greatly
a matter of taste for which there is no accounting." I agree
with him on this point; and, as evidence of what his taste is, let
me make an extract from his description of the discovery of the
locality of the Popham Colony. "Nothing would satisfy a few
excellent people of Maine, but to dig up the sickening remains,
and flaunt them under the nostrils of the community. Here was
an offense against decency and sanitary regulations, indictable
at common law. In cholera times the proceeding is insufferable. Their first mistake was, that when they came to the putrid
mass they did not carefully replace the sod." Does this read
like a review from a student of history? Does it not more
likely resemble the report of a city scavenger, when the cholera
is expected? Then, next, comes a quotation from Lord Bacon's
essays on plantations in general, published about twenty years
after the Popham expedition; and it is difficult to see what it has
to do with the Popham Colony. If it could be referred to any
one in particular, it must have been the then transporting of
such people as he talks of to Virginia. Next, he asserts that the
Colony only occupied "a few acres of ground on the promontory
of Sabino." Will he tell how many more acres were really
occupied at Jamestown or Plymouth the first six months of their
existence?

Then comes a repetition of the old traditionary story published doubtingly by Williamson. A venerable New England writer says, "tradition is the biggest liar in the world," and, in this case, I certainly acquiesce in his assertion, and I doubt if any respectable historian would think of repeating so questionable a tale. In speaking of the end of the colony, by reason of the death of the two Pophams, he says, "did it ever occur to 'Sabino' that his colony must have had a slender foundation to have fallen into ruins at the death of two out of a hundred and twenty persons?" Will he tell us how many more than the death of the two most prominent persons at Plymouth would have. caused its abandonment during their extremity in the spring of 1621? Certainly, not many. Then comes near a column of abuse on the Chief Justice, with abundant extracts from his biographers which may all be true; but, if so, his appointment and continuance on the bench was a disgrace and shame to Queen Elizabeth and the leading men of her reign. And then he comes to that cannon story again. Did it ever occur to him, that, if the statement were true, the returning colonists would have related it at home? For such things always come out; and the Pophamites had as bitter enemies there as P. is, and so it would have been a part of the authentic history of that expedition. Have there not been much worse outrages on the poor Indian all over our country since? And then he repeats his doubts about the arrival of that pretty pinnace in England, of which there can be no more question than of the return of many of the early emigrant ships which carried back passengers who were known to have reached there, while there is no mention of the ships.

But he states "Brief Relation says nothing about the arrival of *either vessel*: it records simply the arrival of *these people* here in England." Well that out-Herods Herod: how does he expect they got there? He certainly knows they embarked in both vessels, for Strachey says, "Wherefore they all ymbarqued in this new arrived ship and in the new pynnace, the Virginia, and set saile for England." Now, I advise this learned pundit to look among his mass of newspapers; and, if he finds the London Shipping List of that time, he may be enlightened. And if he still doubts let him ask the opinion of any of our best writers on New England history, and my word for it he will not find one to indorse his views. One, certainly, whose opinion is of the greatest weight, and as anti-Popham as himself, has given a decided negative to his assertions.

And now comes a long dissertation on the blessings that have been experienced in Maine, by Massachusetts extending its government over it. Some of these moral reflections may be true, but many of the inhabitants of that territory did not then see it. I certainly agree with him in his appreciation of the energy and intelligence of the settlers of Maine and their descendants. They are equal to, and very much resemble, those of the other New England States; but what this has to do with Popham, he don't tell us. And, finally, he undertakes in a note to give the writer of that famous letter about the ship a kick, by stating that a writer in a Portland paper has had his article badly printed by having it done so far from home; and, when revised, he will give it the attention it deserves. Very kind.

Having made a somewhat rapid survey of his three or four heavy columns, "a mighty maze, and yet without a plan," I will look at his famous first attack, or, as the writer in the Portland Advertiser calls it, " the fire of his skirmish line;" and will now give his assertions there a passing notice, glancing over his attack on the Memorial Volume, the defence of Gorges, and his abuse of their authors, who are perfectly able to defend themselves, and may do so hereafter. He talks strongly about "historical verities:" let us see how fairly he treats authentic history. And first, will he tell us where he finds the colonists called "convicted felons," "cowards, Old Bailey convicts and knaves?" and that "they had saved their necks by emigrating," etc., etc.? Can he point to the book and the page for these "historical verities"? He may it is true quote a writer who says "many of them were endangered of the law." So were many of the Plymouth colonists, — to their honor, when we consider what law was, and what protection human rights had under James I.

Again, let us look at his assertions relative to that "pretty pinnace." In his "first consideration," he argues that a sea-worthy vessel was never built by the colonists; and, by inference, would make us believe that it was not built at all, saying "there was not time between the 15th of December and spring to build a sea-worthy vessel,"—when not a person but himself who ever perused "Brief Relation" or "Strachey" doubted the building and sailing for England of such a ship. Next, "that they had no need of a vessel." As if they did not know their own wants better than we do. Can there be much doubt it was the intention of the projectors to have a vessel built, and that for this purpose they sent over "Master Digby and the carpenters"? And then he coolly states she was built of "green pine," and repeatedly calls her a "fishing boat," and implies that she went a fishing. Will he also give his authority for these statements? Every reader of history knows these assertions are untrue; and till he can clear himself of this charge, let him not undertake to lecture others on "historical verities."

It will be seen that I have not noticed his argument relative to the craft built by the French at Port Royal, and which by almost a miracle carried the survivors to their homes; for the reason that we were considering English occupation of New England, and that alone. French enterprise and colonization was an entirely different affair, and had nothing to do with the subject under consideration; and the writer of "the letter" could not fairly have anticipated that it could be made to refer to any but Englishmen. It will also be noticed that I have not undertaken to advocate or indorse the Popham enterprise and its effects in general, but only to show up some of the errors of its opponents. There is and will be a wide difference of opinion on that point; but all will agree that it has been of great benefit to printers, and that they have shed a larger quantity of ink in elucidating these controversies than was lost in blood in "P.'s" imaginary fights with the Indians at Sabino.

Having made a running review of "P.'s" long columns, I would in conclusion offer him some advice, which, I trust, he will receive in the same kind way in which it is given. First, do not fear that Popham history will ever in the slightest way overshadow the lustre of Old Plymouth and Massachusetts Bay. They stand too firm to be shaken: their true glories will continue to brighten and expand through ages yet to come, till they are appreciated and acknowledged throughout the world. Don't look on the very worst side of history: much of it is bad enough at best; and we can hardly read some of the annals of our own ancestors, written by themselves, without a blush. Do not write so ferociously: people are not frightened by ink, particularly Pophamites. "A kind word turneth away wrath." Don't ruin that preface to the reprint which you have had some two years in process of incubation, by bringing Popham and Gorges into it, when there is no occasion for it. And, as a general amnesty, even for the deepest crimes, is the order of the day, you had better accept it on the following cheap terms, viz., as hot weather is approaching, and, if you have not killed out the Pophamites entirely, — and I don't really think you have even ruffled a feather,— they will in August have their picnic celebration at Sabino as usual, now let us both attend. Then, after partaking of their chowder, we will smoke the calumet of peace; drink inspiration — if we can — from that ancient well, but certainly good cool water, and something in it, if you say so; and finally bury the hatchet in the remains of that old ditch, and pledge ourselves to everlasting peace.

JUNE, 1866. SAGADAHOC.

BIBLIOGRAPHY OF THE POPHAM COLONY.

"English Colonization in America. | Public Celebration." A brief sketch of the Colony, and of the proposed Celebration, by Mr. John A. Poor; which was sent to invited guests. July, 1862.

"Historical Celebration at Fort Popham, August 29, 1862." Programme of the Celebration.

"An Order for Morning Prayer" [read by Bishop Burgess]. 8vo, 8 pp.

[Thirty-Four] "Toasts | for the | Historical Celebration. | To be arranged hereafter in appropriate order." 8vo. 4 pp.

CARDS (4½ by 7½ inches) : —

1. Latin Inscription for the Memorial Stone. On the reverse, an English Translation.

2. Latin Inscription as before. On the reverse, " The First Colony | on the Shores of New England | was Founded here, | August 19th, O. S., 1607 | under | George Popham. |

A printed circular headed " Public Historical Celebration," dated August 12, 1862; which was sent to invited guests, with a "Private Explanatory Note," stating that the Celebration "is held under the auspices of the Maine Historical Society, which proposes to. print a full report in the form of a Memorial Volume."

9

NEWSPAPER ARTICLES WITH REFERENCE TO THE FIRST CELE-
BRATION.

Bath Sentinel and Times, July 10, 1862. Mr. B. C. Bailey
recommends calling a public meeting, to make arrangements for
a Celebration.

The same, July 22, 1862. The Mayor of Bath calls the meeting, for Monday, July 28.

The same, July 29. Report of the meeting.

Portland Press, July 30. Report of the meeting, List of Com-
mittees, etc.

Daily Evening Globe, St. John, N.B., August 23, 1862. " The
First English Settlement in New England; " by John Wilkinson.

Portland Advertiser, August 28, 1862. The Order of the
Celebration.

The same, August 30, 1862. An Account of the Celebration;
with Mr. John A. Poor's Oration.

The same, September 3, 1862. Mr. Poor's Oration reprinted
with corrections. Mr. T. D. McGee's Address, and Mr. R.
K. Sewall's Response to a Toast.

Bath Times, September 1, 1862. An Account of the Celebration.

Portland Press, September 6. Mr. John Neal complains of
the arrangements of the Celebration.

Portland Advertiser, September 8. Mr. Charles J. Gilman, the
Chief Marshal, replies.

Portland Transcript, September 4. An account of the Celebration.

Brunswick Telegraph, September 6. An Account of the
Celebration.

Christian Mirror, Portland, September 9. "A Sermon preached
at Phipsburg, Me., on the Sabbath after the Celebration, by Rev.
Francis Norwood."

The same, September 16. Mr. John A. Poor reviews Mr.
Norwood's Sermon.

The same. October 7. " Popham Discussion:" Mr. Norwood replies to Mr. Poor; and "Popham Errata:" Mr. John Wingate Thornton reviews Mr. Poor's article of September 16.

New York Journal of Commerce, November 6. Report of the October Meeting of the New York Historical Society. Remarks concerning the Popham Celebration by Mr. George Folsom and Mr. J. R. Brodhead.

New York Christian Times, November 20. Fuller report of the same.

Boston Evening Traveller, November 21. Correspondence of Rev. William S. Bartlett, of Chelsea. and Prof. Emory Washburn, of Cambridge, concerning the Speech of the latter at the Popham Celebration.

Congregational Quarterly, Boston, April, 1863, Vol. v., p. 143–160. "Colonial Schemes of Popham and Gorges. By John Wingate Thornton, Esq., Boston." A Speech at the First Popham Celebration, with twelve and a half pages of "Notes and Authorities appended as proofs."

A few copies of this article were printed, with the following title page, as

A PAMPHLET. "Colonial Schemes of Popham and Gorges. | Speech | of | John Wingate Thornton, Esq., | at the | Fort Popham Celebration, | August 29, 1862, | under the auspices of the | Maine Historical Society. | Boston. 1863." 8vo, 20 pp. [This Speech is not contained in the Popham "Memorial Volume."]

The above was noticed and discussed in —

North American Review, July 1863, Vol. xcvii., p. 288.
Christian Examiner, July 1863, Vol. lxxv., p. 143.
Historical Collections of the Essex Institute. August, 1863, Vol. v. pp. 175–192; by Mr. A. C. Goodell.
Boston Review, November, 1863, Vol. iii., p. 641.
Historical Magazine, New York. 1863, Vol. vii., p. 231.

Christian Mirror, Portland, April 28, 1863.
Boston Journal, August 11, 1863.
Boston Evening Transcript, April 24. 1863.
Portland Transcript, May 9, 1863.

A PAMPHLET. "The Connection | of the | Church of England | with Early | American Discovery | and | Colonization. | By the Rev. William Stevens Perry, M. A. | Portland, Maine. | 1863." 8vo. 7 pp.

Messrs. Bailey and Noyes, of Portland, Publishers, in April, 1863, issued a circular Prospectus for the publication of the "Memorial Volume;" soliciting Subscriptions.

"MEMORIAL VOLUME | of the | Popham Celebration, | August 29, 1862 : | commemorative of the Planting of the | Popham Colony on the Peninsula of Sabino, | August 19, O. S., 1607, | establishing the Title of England to the Continent. | Published under the direction of the | Rev. Edward Ballard, | Secretary of the Executive Committee of the Celebration. | Portland : | Bailey and Noyes. | 1863." 8vo. 368 pp.

Bound with the same : —

"English Colonization in America. | A | Vindication of the Claims | of | Sir Ferdinando Gorges, | as the | Father of English Colonization in America. | By John A. Poor. | (Delivered before the Historical Societies of Maine, and New York.) | New York : D. Appleton and Company. | 1862." 8vo. [Address, 92 pp. Appendix, 52 pp.,] 144 pp.

"Popham Celebration | at | Sabino, | August, 1863." Programme in broadside.

The Popham Celebration of August 29, 1863, Mr. George Folsom, Orator, was reported in —

Portland Daily Advertiser, August 31, 1863.
Portland Daily Press, August 31, and September 3, 1863.

Brunswick Telegraph, September 4, 1863.
Boston Witness and Advocate, September 11, 1863.
Boston Courier. September 2, 1863.
Portland Daily Press. September 30, 1863: "Popham — Settlement — Memorial and Celebrations." Signed " P." [Mr. George Prince.]

A PAMPHLET. " The Beginning of America | A | Discourse | delivered before the | New York Historical Society | on its Fifty-ninth Anniversary | Tuesday November 17 1863 | By | Erastus C. Benedict | New York | 1864." 8vo, 64 pp.

Portland Daily Press, January 29, 1864. Notice of Meeting of the Maine Historical Society, and of Judge Bourne's Reply to Mr. Thornton's Pamphlet.

A PAMPHLET. " An | Address | on the | Character of the Colony | founded by | George Popham, | at the | Mouth of the Kennebec River August 19th [O. S.] 1607. | Delivered in Bath, | on the Two hundred and fifty-seventh Anniversary | of that Event. | By Hon. Edward E. Bourne, | of Kennebunk. | Delivered and Published at the request of the Committee on the Commemoration. | Portland: | 1864." 8vo, 60 pp.

The above was noticed and discussed in —
Christian Mirror. Portland, February 21, 1865.
Boston Evening Transcript, February 13, 1865 ; by Rev. George E. Ellis, D.D.
Bath Daily Sentinel and Times, August 30, 31, September 1, 1864.
The same, March 16, 1865. "Fort Popham Colony."
The same, March 16, 1865. " The Popham Settlement;" by Rev. Edward Ballard.
The same, March 30, 1865.
The same. July 7, 1865.

Boston Daily Advertiser, August 4, 1866: Report of the Meeting of the Maine Historical Society of August 2, containing a letter by Mr. John A. Poor, with regard to new evidences found in Carayon's Relations.

The Popham Celebration of August 29, 1866, was reported iu *Boston Daily Advertiser,* September 1, 1866.

Boston Journal, September 1, 1866.

New York Times, September 4, 1866.

New York Christian Intelligencer, September, 1866.

Brunswick Telegraph, September 14, 1866.

A Pamphlet. "The Popham Colony | A Discussion of its Historical Claims | With a | Bibliography of the Subject | Boston | Wiggin and Lunt 13 School Street 1866 " 8vo, 72 pp.

www.ingramcontent.com/pod-product-compliance
Lightning Source LLC
Chambersburg PA
CBHW022152090426
42742CB00010B/1489